Clash of Ideals

CASES
IN
AMERICAN
POLITICAL
DEVELOPMENT

Clash of Ideals

CASES
IN
AMERICAN
POLITICAL
DEVELOPMENT

Brendan J. Doherty
Howard R. Ernst
Stephen E. Frantzich
Priscilla H. Machado Zotti

All, UNITED STATES NAVAL ACADEMY

LANAHAN PUBLISHERS, INC.   *Baltimore*

The text of this book was composed in Bembo
with display type in Garamond and Bernhard Modern.
Composition by BYTHEWAY PUBLISHING SERVICES
Manufacturing by GASCH PRINTING

Grateful acknowledgment is extended to the Rhode Island
Historical Society for permitting Howard R. Ernst to adapt
his essay from "A Call to Arms: Thomas Wilson Dorr's
Forceful Effort to Implement the People's Constitution,"
Rhode Island History. Rhode Island Historical Society, Fall
2008; and to Peter Lang Publishing for permitting Priscilla H.
Machado Zotti to adapt her essay from *Injustice for All: Mapp
vs. Ohio and the Fourth Amendment*, New York: Peter Lang
Publishing, 2005.

ISBN-10 1-930398-13-1
ISBN-13 978-1-930398-13-9

LANAHAN PUBLISHERS, INC.
324 Hawthorne Road, Baltimore, MD 21210
1–866–345–1949 [Toll Free]
LANAHAN@AOL.COM
WWW.LANAHANPUBLISHERS.COM

5 6 7 8 9 0

CONTENTS

PREFACE

THE AMERICAN POLITICAL SYSTEM has evolved over time, with each generation guiding and molding the course of American political development. This book is written from the perspective that "The Founding" did not end in 1776, when the former Colonies declared their independence from the British throne, or even in 1789, when the States united behind their newly minted Constitution. This work presents the American political system as a dynamic river—a river that constantly flows, eroding obstacles, and continuously interacting with the political landscape along its way.

To equate American political development to a river is not to suggest that its course is predictable or placid. While the American system has gathered considerable momentum over time, it has regularly faced formidable obstacles, each pushing the nation in an unpredictable direction, each fundamentally altering the course of American political history. Some of these challenges are well known and engrained in the American psyche, such as the Boston

Tea Party, Shays's Rebellion, the Civil War, the Great Depression, the Cold War, the Civil Rights Movement, and the threat of terrorism. But there are also less well known moments in American political development that have also profoundly influenced the nation's political course. This book focuses on several carefully selected and long neglected American stories, with the idea that it is often more useful to consider important themes through unfamiliar stories than it is to search for new meaning in familiar narratives. We hope that readers will consider each case with a clear head and a fresh perspective. The cases were also selected because each story embodies a core dilemma. In each case essential governing principles—principles that are central to the American experience—either pull the system in competing directions or collide with an explosive impact. The cases reveal that nothing is more influential to American political development than when its core principles come in conflict.

The chapters in this book explore the details of each case, showing both the personal side of the stories as well as the contextual factors that influenced the outcomes. It is in the particulars that the careful reader can find the universal. Moreover, the cases address American political development at different times, with two cases addressing 19th century confrontations (the presidential elections of 1824 and 1828, and the Dorr War of 1842), one case firmly grounded in the mid-20th century (the Mapp case) and one case addressing issues of congressional representation in the 20th and early 21st centuries.

The cases were also selected because they span the major institutions of American government: Part One addresses constitutional issues; Part Two focuses on legislative questions; Part Three explores the executive; and Part Four investigates a judicial theme. Together, the works bring to life several important but largely unheralded episodes that provide students with a novel approach to better understand the factors that continue to influence the development of the American political system.

We would like to thank Don Fusting of Lanahan Publishers, Inc. for recognizing the value of the project and for editing our work. Brendan Doherty would like to thank Robyn Altman for her comments and suggestions regarding the presidential elections chapter. Howard Ernst would like to thank Russell J. DeSimone, Bill McQuade, John Pierzynski, and the professional staffs of the John Hay Library, Rhode Island State Archives, and Rhode Island Historical Society for assisting his research on the Dorr Rebellion. He would also like to thank Jeff Anderson, Paul Bolt, Russell Brown, Paul Carrese, Tracey Ernst, Kevin Haney, Deron Jackson, Shawn Loughman, Kenneth Middleton, Mauricio Monte, Tom Mowle, Melissa Stango, and Heather Waldorf for reviewing drafts of the essay. Dr. Ernst extends a special thank you to Dorr Rebellion authority Dr. Patrick T. Conley and to Dr. Hillard Beller for their invaluable comments and suggestions. Lastly, Dr. Ernst would like to thank Dr. Elizabeth C. Stevens, editor of *Rhode Island History,* for allowing portions of his earlier essay about the Dorr War to be reprinted in this publication.

We would also like to note that the authors have agreed to accept no royalties for the publication of this work or compensation of any kind from the publisher. This work is written for the benefit our American government students, who have committed themselves to protecting and strengthening the American political system and who recognize that a solid understanding of American political development is essential to that end. We dedicate this book to our students, the Midshipmen of the United States Naval Academy.

BRENDAN J. DOHERTY
HOWARD R. ERNST
STEPHEN E. FRANTZICH
PRISCILLA H. MACHADO ZOTTI
Annapolis, Maryland
February 2009

Clash of Ideals

CASES

IN

AMERICAN

POLITICAL

DEVELOPMENT

PART ONE

FOUNDING IDEALS

Popular Sovereignty vs. Rule of Law—The Dorr War of 1842

HOWARD R. ERNST

On its surface, the Dorr Rebellion[1] is an interesting story about an obscure 19th century voting rights rebellion. But beneath the veneer, it reveals much more: it shows the inherent tensions that define popular governance—the very tensions that bind representative democracy and that threaten to tear it apart at its seams. At its core it is about the struggle to create and maintain a governmental system that respects the will of the people and that governs wisely, that provides law and order, but not at the expense of civil liberties and civil rights. Looking back in history, we see that this rebellion marked the final chapter in America's "revolutionary period," more accurately, an epilogue to the American Revolution. Born from the fires of revolution against a colonial master and monarchical system, the glow of rebellion had cooled by the mid–19th century. The young nation witnessed the suppression of Shays's Rebellion and the Whiskey Rebellion. By the outbreak of the Dorr Rebellion, the nation was rethinking the virtue of armed conflict as a legitimate tool for promoting domestic change. Looking forward, we see that the rebellion was a vital first step in the nation's long struggle to win civil rights for its disenfranchised majority. Following in Dorr's wake were the nation's aboli-

tionists who resisted the institution of slavery and the disenfranchise-
ment of former slaves, the radical suffragists of the early 20th century,
the civil rights activists of the 1960s, and the Hispanic protesters of
the 21st century, who are just now beginning their struggle for politi-
cal rights. In the post-9/11 world, where the federal government has
asserted vast powers in the name of national security, the lessons of
the Dorr Rebellion take on new meaning. The natural tension be-
tween security and liberty, which defined the Dorr conflict, has be-
come a defining theme of the current context. Long before there was a
Patriot Act, a federal wire-tapping program, or secret CIA prisons,
the citizens of Rhode Island were subject to martial law, the threat of
federal troops, and the scrutiny of federal spies. While the threats to-
day are different, the justification for government intervention remains
the same. Once again government officials are calling on Americans
to sacrifice civil liberty in the name of security. While the Dorr War
tells the story of an obscure voting rights rebellion, it also gives in-
sights into 21st century America. It is a single iteration in human-
kind's continuous struggle to achieve legitimate and effective gover-
nance.

THE INSURGENTS WHO REPORTED for battle were tired,
impatient, and anxious. Some of the two hundred and fifty com-
batants were simply fatigued by the late hour, while others felt the
effect of hard spirits. The working-class insurgents could wait no
longer for their promised reinforcements; soon the sun would rise
and rob them of their protective cover. As the men left their headquarters, they did so to the sound of the city's church bells. Three
strokes of the bell echoed throughout the tension-filled morning
air, signaling the residents of Providence that the insurgents were
in motion.[2]

Behind their leader, Thomas Wilson Dorr, the armed men
snaked through the city's streets, traveled west on Atwells Avenue,
then south on Love Lane, past Broadway and High Street, making
their way to Cranston Street and eventually to the target of their
attack—Providence's highly fortified arsenal. While not the most
direct route, the path kept the men out of the area's back alleys and

reduced the chance of a successful ambush. The circuitous route added about fifteen minutes to the march and provided Dorr's men an opportunity to clear their heads after a long night of anxiously awaiting the attack.

It seemed inevitable that the final vote in this matter would be cast with bullets and not ballots—that it would take place in pitch darkness, under a heavy fog. Dorr and his most devout followers viewed the fog-induced darkness as a blessing, as it provided cover for their attack in a battlefield that afforded few natural protections. One insurgent described the darkness this way, "The night was not chosen because it was dark; the fog came up late; it seemed like an interposition of Divine Providence" (qtd. in Burke's Report 907). Divine providence or not, the fog also provided a cloak for the timid, behind which they could hide their natural fears and through which they could retreat should things prove difficult.

On the other side of its stone walls, the defenders of the arsenal assumed their defensive positions. Most of the defenders stationed themselves near the windows on the building's second level, which afforded them an unobstructed line of fire and added protection over those on the lower level. The defenders understood that Dorr's cannons would be aimed at the arsenal's lower doors. It would be through the iron doors that the insurgents would rush the arsenal, and it was here that the most ardent defenders positioned themselves.

On the vulnerable lower level was Dorr's brother-in-law, Quartermaster General Ames (Mowry, *The Dorr War* 184). Also in among the defenders of the arsenal that night were Dorr's two uncles, Zachariah Allen and Crawford Allen, as well as his younger brother, Sullivan Dorr. Thomas Dorr's own father, Sullivan Dorr, Sr, while not stationed at the arsenal, did report to the Charter side for active duty against his son (Gettleman 7; Conley 340; and Hodges 189). A disagreement that divided a state and captured the attention of the nation now split a family to its core and threatened to unleash unimaginable energy. In the early morning of May 18, 1842, Thomas Dorr gave the order to fire on the state arsenal, declaring war on his friends, his family, and the state that he loved.

A Clash of Ideals

The crisis arose from a conflict over voting rights and political representation. As other states were expanding suffrage in the early 19th century, voting rights in Rhode Island had become increasingly restricted. Conservative government officials passed laws limiting political participation to "freeholders" (white males) of sizeable estates and allowed the state's legislative districts to become grossly malapportioned, giving disproportionate influence to landowners in rural areas. By the election of 1840, the majority of the state's legislative seats were selected by the votes of just 3,149 freeholders from over-represented regions (Burke's Report 11). The once-democratic settlement, with political freedoms to match its well-known religious freedoms, had become a severely limited democracy.

Leaders within the state's conservative legislature made no apologies for the political inequalities that had developed. They argued that political privilege was the rightful outcome of societal standing, not a wrong to be corrected. For men like Benjamin Hazard, a leading member of the legislature, the protection of political liberty and the establishment of law and order was the best measure of governmental merit, not the number of people who could vote or the extent to which governments adhered to abstract ideals. Hazard and his followers believed that there were two distinct classes of people—those who were qualified to govern and those who were better off being governed. The conservatives were determined to keep government control in the "sound part of the community" (qtd. in Burke's Report 378).

In the eyes of the state's disenfranchised majority, a political class system had emerged, where landless laborers were required to pay taxes and serve in the militia, while the privileged class of "freemen" controlled the political system. To them, the state had degenerated into a political oligarchy. Trusting in the public will more than the state's established authority, a group of reformers, led by Thomas Dorr, moved forward with a radical plan to expand suffrage and to replace the existing government with a constitutionally elected alternative. Like the nation's founders in 1776, the Rhode Island insurgents of 1842 were determined to assert their right to popular sovereignty, even if it meant engaging in a bloody war.

Below the surface, the conflict was about far more than voting rights. It was nothing less than the outward manifestation between competing views of legitimate government, between two distinct political traditions. The crisis forced the state's residents to swear allegiance to one of two competing rulers and in so doing to declare their faith either in the collective voice of the people or the sanctity of the existing laws. The conflict promised to settle, at least temporarily, the unfinished business of the American founding. Its participants aimed to determine where the accent should fall in *representative democracy*—either on representation or on democracy. At its core, it was a struggle to define the very nature of democracy in America.

The warring factions based their claims on time-tested political beliefs. For the conservatives and their law-based tradition, governance was solemn business, appropriate for only the most capable members of society. Governing was reserved for statesmen, the high priests of civil society, chosen by the society's elite class. While the conservatives agreed that it would be ideal if all members of society possessed the civic virtue that makes wise government possible, they saw little evidence that such an arrangement ever existed or was even possible. Experience taught them that the masses were unworthy guardians of liberty and were primarily driven by self-interest. The conservatives put their faith in the wisdom of the few, rather than the demands of the multitude. Through careful study and sincere deliberation, men of the highest character were sought to overcome the chains of self-interest. The intent of the law was not to reflect mass opinion, what the conservatives considered mob-rule, but to guide the public's actions. For the conservatives, laws established rules that enabled the masses to behave virtuously, regardless of their degraded state. Not confident in the moral strength of the average citizen, the conservatives stressed the importance of adhering to the rule of law and gave primacy to the civic virtues that promoted lawful behavior. Self-control and duty were their guiding principles. Civic obedience was the primary demand of civil society. The peace the conservatives sought was that of *Pax Romana* (the peace of Rome)—the peace and stability that is achieved through surrendering to the law. The cement that bound society, according to this tradition, was formed from a combination of sound laws and a loyal citizenry. Those who strayed from the law, like the Rhode Island reformers turned insurgents, threatened society's very foundation and were treated accordingly.

The reformers, in contrast, followed in the footsteps of Thomas Jefferson, Patrick Henry, and Samuel Adams. Their tradition stressed the sanctity that lies in the heart of all individuals and the innate moral sense that guides and dignifies human action. Their philosophy was rooted in the central belief that all people, regardless of their status in society, possess a divine spark, and that taken collectively, the voice of the people is the purest reflection of the voice of the Almighty (*vox populi, vox Dei*).

The supporters of expanded suffrage did not prefer democratic governance out of convenience or self-interest; they worshipped at a different civic altar than the conservatives. For them, democratic government, rooted in popular sovereignty, was the only form of government capable of dignifying the human spirit. Civic virtue was not achieved through blind obedience to the law, especially laws that were created to control rather than reflect the public will. On the contrary, true civic virtue was achieved by adhering to the collective wisdom that gives law its moral force and government its political legitimacy.

The differences between the two groups were based on different civic covenants. The conservatives' covenant was carved in stone, passed down through a chosen medium to the average person; the reformer's was etched in the hearts of society's lowest and highest members. At best, the traditions were distant cousins, each claiming elements rooted in the American political tradition. But in mid-19th century Rhode Island, the traditions had grown incompatible.

By the spring of 1842, the competing factions within Rhode Island had torn the tiny state asunder. The state was now governed by competing legal systems, rival governors, and separate legislative assemblies. One government, referred to as the People's Government, was led by Thomas Dorr. Dorr and his radical followers founded their government on the ideal of popular sovereignty and organized under a state constitution that was ratified by an unauthorized popular referendum the previous winter. The other government, led by Governor King, was referred to as the Charter Government. King's government received its authority from the state's original royal Charter, which the state had failed to replace with a modern constitution after severing ties with England. The Charter Government justified its authority, not on popular consent, but on the legitimacy that came with nearly two hundred years of relatively stable and prosperous governance. Both governments claimed to be the legitimate authority of the state, and the supporters of each side, including armed militias, swore to defend their respective governments.

An Unlikely Revolutionary

Thomas Wilson Dorr has been described as an unlikely revolutionary. Charles Congdon, a pro-Dorr newspaperman at the time of the uprising, remembered his first encounter with Dorr. "He sat calmly smoking a cigar, looking, I must say, as little like an incendiary and revolutionist as any man whom I have ever encountered" (109). Dorr was the eldest son of one of the state's most influential couples. His father, Sullivan Dorr, had risen from modest circumstances to build a considerable fortune through foreign trade. His mother, Lydia Allen Dorr, could trace her Rhode Island lineage back to William Harris, one of Roger Williams's original followers who helped settle the state in 1636. Sullivan Dorr's wealth, coupled with Lydia Dorr's social standing, combined to provide Thomas Dorr all the advantages that came with patrician privilege in 19th-century New England.

Dorr received the best education available to a young man of means, attending Phillips-Exeter Academy and Harvard College.[3] He arrived at Harvard in 1819 at the tender age of fourteen. Rather than engage in the pranks and mischief of his classmates, he developed a reputation as a serious student—a mathematician no less. In 1820, when the campus was embroiled in controversy after two students were disciplined for unruly behavior and nearly all of Dorr's classmates temporarily left the campus in protest, Dorr stayed in Cambridge and continued his studies. He was subsequently "black listed" by his classmates, accused of being a spy for the administration, and had his shower stall removed from his dorm room and burned on the college yard. By the time the student unrest subsided, forty-two of Dorr's seventy classmates were expelled from Harvard, but not Thomas Dorr, who was one of the few students from his class to graduate on schedule (Gettleman 13; Morison, "The Great Rebellion" 64–95; and Morison, *Three Centuries of Harvard* 230–231).

After graduating from Harvard, he studied law in New York under the direction of two of the nation's leading legal minds: Chancellor James Kent and Vice Chancellor William T. McCoun (Gettleman 15). He was admitted to the Rhode Island state bar in 1827 and was elected to the General Assembly at the age of twenty-nine. Everything in Dorr's background suggested that he would continue along his privileged path and take his place within the state's ruling class.

In his thirties Dorr found his political voice. He became a champion for religious freedom and public education. He also argued against imprisonment for debtors and the institution of slavery (Gettleman 17–18). His passion, however, was spent working for the expansion of voting rights and for the adoption of a modern constitution.

While he was generally considered affable and held in high regard for his intellectual prowess, he was also a notoriously stubborn idealist. Almon Hodges, a contemporary of Dorr's who knew him well, described Dorr as "agreeable and genial socially," but also "self willed and headstrong" (176). Congdon, Dorr's ally in the reform movement, joked that Dorr's opponents described him as possessing "boundless obstinacy, which his admirers called firmness" (108). Beneath his genteel veneer was a combination of moral certainty and intellectual strength that led to unwavering political principles.

His holy trinity of democratic governance included the ideals of *popular sovereignty* (i.e., the belief that all legitimate political power is derived from the consent of the governed and that the governed have a right and duty to replace governmental institutions that fail to secure the common good), *equal representation* (i.e., the notion that no citizen or group of citizens should be barred from the political process for arbitrary or unimportant reasons, and that governmental institutions should be representative of the citizenry), and *limited government* (i.e., the idea that the scope of governmental influence, particularly in areas of individual conscience, should be limited and well-defined by the law).

His hope to foster reform through the existing political system was dashed in 1837 when Dorr suffered a resounding political blow. That year Dorr ran for the U.S. Congress as member of the Constitutional Party and received an embarrassingly small percent of the vote. Having had his reform message repudiated by the eligible voters, he swore off the reform movement, concluding that he would only return to the effort when the disenfranchised voters took up the cause.

In the early 1840s, the state's disenfranchised masses did organize for change, and true to his word, Dorr returned to the reform effort. The new movement was far larger and more radical than the one that Dorr had led the previous decade. Built from a wave of popular support and righteous indignation, it had momentum of its own, propelling Dorr in a direction that he could not have anticipated. Before the crisis would end, Dorr, the principled young man from Harvard, who had stayed true to his studies while his classmates rebelled, would prove that he was willing to die so that others might attain the political rights he already enjoyed.

The Parched Political Landscape

While Dorr eventually came to lead the rebellion, the uprising had roots that predated his involvement, roots that could be traced back to one of the nation's earliest and most significant political dilemmas—who in society should be eligible to participate in the political process? This single question lies at the heart of many of the nation's most tumultuous conflicts—the American Revolution, the Civil War, the women's suffrage movement, the Civil Rights Movement, the immigration crisis of the 21st century, and, of course, the Rhode Island Rebellion of 1842. Essentially, it pits those who view political participation as a privilege, reserved for a certain class of citizen, against those who view it as a birthright, enjoyed by all competent members of a free society.

The U.S. Constitution does not specify the voter qualifications for participating in U.S. House elections and makes no mention of electoral qualifications for other branches of government, as the House was the only federal institution that was originally chosen directly by the people. Article One, Section Two of the U.S. Constitution reads, "The House of Representatives shall be composed of Members chosen every second Year by the People of the several States, and the Electors in each State shall have the Qualifications requisite for Electors of the most numerous Branch of the State Legislature."

The Constitution's silence regarding voter qualifications does not suggest the issue was of little importance or that it was not debated at the Constitutional Convention. On the contrary, conservatives like Gouverneur Morris of Pennsylvania, argued that voting rights should be reserved for a privileged few. "Children do not vote. Why? Because they want prudence, because they have no will of their own. The ignorant & the dependent can be little trusted with the public interest" (qtd. in Madison 402–403). Morris and other supporters of limited suffrage based their arguments on the aristocratic ideal that those with the most at stake in society (i.e., those who had achieved an elevated standing in society) were best qualified to hold public office and to participate in elections. When this line of argument proved unpersuasive to more moderate observers, the supporters of restricted suffrage warned that "people who have no property" will sell their votes "to the rich who will be able to buy them." In either case, the supporters of restricted voting rights deemed the poor "unfit guardians of liberty" (Morris qtd. in Madison 402).

During the Constitutional debates, those opposed to property requirements and other political restrictions tended to argue from a pragmatic position. Some feared that a national standard would weaken support for the Constitution, as it would inevitably restrict suffrage in states in which the right to vote was already widely enjoyed. On this point, Pierce Butler, Delegate from South Carolina, warned that "there is no right of which people are more jealous than that of suffrage" (qtd. in Madison 402). Oliver Ellsworth, Delegate from Connecticut, was concerned that voting requirements based on the ownership of land would unfairly work against merchants and manufacturers (qtd. in Madison 402). Others were concerned that the sons of farmers, who worked family farms but did not own them, would be unfairly excluded (Madison 404). Still others feared the confusion that a national standard could cause, as it could lead to one set of suffrage requirements for the national legislature and a second set of requirements for state and local offices (Madison 401). Benjamin Franklin, America's great pragmatist, argued against a property requirement by explaining that one of the reasons that American seamen acted with more valor and patriotism than their British counterparts during the American Revolution was related to "the different manner in which the common people were treated in America and Great Britain" (qtd. in Madison 404).

In the end, the issue proved too prickly to be resolved at the Constitutional Convention. Instead, the founders deferred to the states. Madison reminded the delegates of the dangers of such an approach, as he predicted that "in future times a great majority of the people will not only be without [land] . . . but any other sort of property" (403). Madison knew that the compromise had only postponed the political battle over suffrage. If the republic was to stay true to its founding ideals, suffrage would have to expand to reflect the changing population.

Rhode Island, like the other colonies turned states, developed its own set of laws related to suffrage.[4] Enacted by the Assembly in 1664, Rhode Island's first law limiting suffrage rights specified that "it is also the pleasure and appointment of this General Assembly, that none presume to vote, in the matters aforesaid, but such whom this General Assembly expressly by their writing shall admit as freemen" (Burke's Report 8). The next year the Assembly further specified that voting was to be limited to those "of competent estates, civil conversation, and obedient to the civil magistrate" (Burke's Report 8–9)," introducing the first mention of a property requirement and leaving voting rights to be determined by officials who possessed their own biases and political preferences.

It was most likely an attempt to reduce the arbitrary nature of determining voter eligibility that led to the more specific land-owning requirement that was instituted in 1723. That year the Rhode Island Assembly passed a law limiting political participation to "freeholders of land" valued at "one hundred pounds, or to the value of forty shillings per annum" (Burke's Report 9). The law went on to grant voting rights to the eldest sons of freeholders, establishing the right of primogeniture (Burke's Report 9; Dennison 14–15; and McDougall 47). The amount of property required for voting fluctuated over the next seventy-five years, until 1798 (McDougall 35; Burke's Report 9–10) when the Assembly fixed the amount at $134 and retained the law extending suffrage to the eldest sons of freemen.[5] These qualifications remained in place through the early 1840s and eventually fueled the conflict that erupted in 1842.

Supporters of the restrictions argued that owning a sizable estate served as a proxy for political merit, suggesting a citizen had gained a sufficient interest in the affairs of state and was adequately informed in political matters to warrant the privilege of participation. One supporter of the requirement explained, "We know, therefore, of no better general rule by which to regulate the right of suffrage, than the rule which requires that most probable evidence of permanent interest and attachment which is furnished by the ownership of property" (Hazard qtd. in Burke's Report 383).

Those who met the requirement were given the status of "freemen" and were entitled to full political rights, including the right to vote, hold office, serve on juries, and gain access to the court system for the recovery of debt. While supporters of the property requirement conceded that owning property was "not proof of the possession of virtue or patriotism," supporters argued it was the best available indicator (Hazard qtd. in Burke's Report 385). They also argued that the requirement was fair, since all members of the state who would otherwise be eligible to vote could gain access to the polls through the acquisition of wealth[6] and because the practice was, for the most part, free from the whims and prejudices of local officials.[7]

Opponents to the property requirement took a different position. They held that it was an arbitrary distinction, no more meaningful than considering "physical strength, or mechanical skill, or, in fact, any other quality or thing." For them, "it is plain . . . that no qualities or possessions, which attach to the person, can be the measure of power in the government" (qtd. in Burke's Report 42). They also had serious practical concerns. The opponents feared that citizens were using fraudulent deeds to qualify to vote, a practice that was believed to account for one-quarter of the voters in some towns (King 23–24). If this fear was justified, as it most likely was, the property requirement was not limiting voting rights to the state's most qualified citizens, as the proponents of the land requirement argued. It was actually having the opposite effect; it over-represented the state's least honest citizens.

The land requirement did more than limit suffrage rights. The requirement also limited the legal rights of non-property owners. Without the sponsorship of a landholder, non-landowners were denied access to the courts for the collection of debt and other civil matters. Non-landholders were barred from serving on juries, which in practice denied them the right of a trial by their peers (King 26; McDougall 48; and Burke's Report 13). And to add insult to injury, non-landholders were required to perform military duties, as well as pay taxes to the state. In short, only landowners were given control of the reins of government, but all were required to pull their own weight.

While both sides held that government should be controlled by "the people"—a key tenet of popular sovereignty—they disagreed over the definition "of the people." The Charter side clung to a strict legal definition that limited popular sovereignty to "freemen." For them, government was the equivalent of a corporation in which shareholders (freemen) were granted influence and non-shareholders were excluded from the business of government. The reformers held a more ambitious definition of "the people," which included property holders and non-property holders alike.

By 1840, the voter eligibility rate among the state's adult white male population had dropped to forty-two percent,[8] with disenfranchisement most acute around the sprawling industrial center of Providence (Gettleman 7). A political class system had emerged, where landless laborers were required to pay taxes and serve in the militia if called, while the privileged class of "freemen" and their eldest sons controlled the political system, leading many disenfranchised residents to conclude that the state was being governed by an ever-shrinking political oligarchy.

A Reform Movement Ignites

Thomas Dorr and the supporters of reform were faced with a monumental political challenge. The expansion of suffrage could only be achieved through the Rhode Island Assembly, which was elected by Rhode Island's property-owning elite. The issue of malapportionment (e.g., the problem of legislative districts of vastly different sizes) could only be rectified by amending the royal Charter, a process for which there was no legal basis or precedent. In other words, meaningful political reform would require action by the "aristocrats," the reformers' word for those who benefited from the state's existing political inequality. To reform the system meant to disrupt the state's balance of power and would require the ruling minority to relinquish its privileged position, a fact that was not lost on the frustrated reformers.

Despite all odds, the reformers made several attempts to pressure the Assembly to expand suffrage and to adopt a modern state constitution.[9] Between 1797 and 1834 there were seven different proposals circulated within the Assembly to address the state's constitutional dilemma, each of which failed. By 1840, Dorr, who had led the most recent reform effort, concluded that as long as the constitutional reform process was in the hands of those who benefited from its inequalities, meaningful reform would be blocked indefinitely.

The raucous presidential election of 1840 helped to remind many of the state's residents of their political impotence and served as a catalyst for action (Gettleman 31–35). The election, considered by many to be the nation's first modern presidential contest, was one of the first in which candidates aggressively took their message to the voters and generated an unprecedented level of national excitement. The presidential campaign produced the memorable slogan "Tippecanoe and Tyler too," intended to remind voters of William Henry Harrison's role in the Battle of Tippecanoe during the War of 1812. There was a nationwide political party in progress, complete with parades, log cabins, and hard cider. And Rhode Islanders, for the most part, were not invited (Gettleman 36–37). The election forced Rhode Island's disenfranchised majority to face their political predicament.

Feeding on the excitement generated by the 1840 presidential race, the Rhode Island suffrage movement changed its tone and approach. Rather than risk further humiliation and defeat at the hands of the "ruffled-shirt gentry" within the Assembly, the reformers developed a grassroots strategy and decided to take their case directly to the sovereign people (Hodges 177). In May of 1840, reformers from Providence organized the Rhode Island Suffrage Association, which was soon followed by the creation of numerous local associations throughout the state.[10] The suffrage associations became the embodiment of the cause, giving form to popular sovereignty's persuasive call and providing the ritual and pageantry that is necessary to sustain a civic creed. Unlike the earlier reform efforts that were dominated by progressive members of the Assembly,[11] the suffrage associations were primarily formed by the state's disenfranchised working class (Conley 295; Gettleman 21–22; and Dennison 14–15). The associations were born from profound frustration, as the state's disenfranchised majority witnessed the petitions of their moderate leaders sacrificed, one after the other, at the altar of the established authority. Their arguments were the raw arguments of mechanics and roughnecks. The preamble of the Rhode Island Suffrage Association set the tone of the movement, its members knew their rights "and knowing, dared maintain them."[12]

In its early stages, the Suffrage Association borrowed heavily from the populist techniques of the recent presidential election, holding mass rallies, including marching bands, fiery public speakers, bonfires, pounds of beef, and a steady flow of root beer. The first mass rally was held in Providence, on April 17, 1841, shortly after the Assembly had rejected the reformers' latest petition for a written constitution.[13] An estimated three thousand participants, or roughly three percent of the state's population, participated in the rally. With its parade of butchers, mechanics, and other working

class members, the Providence mass meeting set the stage for future action.[14] The participants paraded under banners that read, "I
Die for Liberty" and "Peacefully If We Can, Forcibly If We Must"
(Burke's Report 663). The rowdy event culminated with lively
speeches and a formal declaration of principles.

The participants ultimately decided that "the two most important objects to be gained in the formation of a constitution are
equal representation and a liberal extension of suffrage" (qtd. in
Burke's Report 404). While less eloquent than Thomas Jefferson's
declaration of 1776, their message was essentially the same—political legitimacy is derived from the consent of the governed and the
majority of Rhode Islanders no longer gave their consent.

By the third mass meeting, convened on July 5, 1841, on a
military training field adjacent to the state arsenal in Providence,
the tone had turned decidedly revolutionary. Dorr and his allies
turned their emphasis from protest to a plan of action. The resolutions passed at this meeting asserted that it was not only the "right,
but the duty" of citizens to assert control over their government
(Burke's Report 408). The Dorrites resolved to hold a convention
for the purpose of drafting a written constitution and "solemnly
pledged" to each other to carry it into effect "by all necessary
means" (Burke's Report 408). One speaker at the July 5th mass
meeting expressed the revolutionary sentiment this way (William
Balch qtd. Conley 303–304).

> Call it a revolution that we say intelligence, virtue, honor,
> patriotism makes the man and not dirt and primogeniture? Call
> it a revolution that we level every false distinction, every grade
> not based on talent or moral worth, and proclaim liberty and
> rights to the people? Then we are revolutionists and glory in it;
> and we will rejoice when such a revolution is consummated and
> its blessings all revealed!

As the movement took shape in the spring and summer of
1841, the calls for action put forth at the rallies became more radi-

cal and more urgent. Participants at pro-suffrage rallies were debating whether or not to refuse military service in the Charter Government, which would have been a violation of state law (Mowry, *The Dorr War* 61). More ominously, the reformers debated whether it was advisable to form independent military units, which would be put to service should the need for military resistance arise (Mowry, *The Dorr War* 61–62). By the summer of 1841, things were becoming far more serious as at least one procession included a parade of armed participants (Gettleman 40).

The reformers' speeches had a sense of urgency that harkened to the spirit of 1776 (Gettleman 18–22) and to the ideals upon which the nation was founded. Their democratic revival was based on the righteousness of their cause. To them, the "high and indomitable spirit of liberty, which GOD breathed into the soul of man . . . This spirit was awake—is awake" (McDougall 115). To the reformers, their cause was not only fair, it was right. They proclaimed that "men, whom God, himself, created, without permission of the General Assembly of Rhode Island" (McDougall 200) were subject to a higher law—natural law.

On July 24, 1841, Thomas Dorr and the other leaders of the suffrage movement went forward with their radical plan and called for a state constitutional convention to be held in the fall (Burke's Report 16; Gettleman 43–44). Delegates to the convention were elected in August, chosen by property holders and non-property holders. The convention convened on the first Monday in October, with Thomas Dorr and the other elected delegates deliberating for five days before producing the People's Constitution (Mowry, *The Dorr War* 70–74). The proposed constitution corrected the state's malapportionment problem and greatly expanded suffrage by removing the state's land-owning requirement.

The People's Constitution was ratified by referendum in a December election, approved by a majority of all voters, as well as a majority of the voters eligible to vote under the restrictive Charter rules (Burke's Report 17). According to the rules established by the new constitution, a second round of elections was scheduled to take place in April and the new government, which would most certainly be led by Dorr, was scheduled to take office on May 3, 1842. For the reformers, the inauguration marked the culmination of years of struggle and the triumph of popular sovereignty, for the Charter Government the inauguration was seen as an act of treason, and they vowed to block it.

The Law and Order Side Resists

One of the most forceful champions of the established order was Benjamin Hazard, a leading conservative who was elected to the Rhode Island Assembly sixty-two consecutive times before retiring (Conley 301). According to Hazard and his allies, the key to wise governance was to limit political participation to the state's wisest statesmen—to those with souls of gold. And since the human soul is forever hidden from human eyes, the conservatives concluded that there was no better measure of political worth than one's position in society. Disproportionate political influence was the reward for social status and the key to wise governance.

In a committee report produced by the Assembly in 1829, Hazard explained that his committee had no intention to "degrade the elective franchise by stripping it of all its necessary qualifications and guards" (qtd. in Burke's Report 391). He also made clear that "there are some who pretend to consider the right of suffrage as an inherent, natural right, which every man ought to enjoy . . . it is not" (qtd. in Burke's Report 381). Electoral safeguards, Hazard argued, were necessary to shield the political system from the influence of the lower sort, such as immigrants "a great majority of whom were, in their own country, in as degraded a condition as men can be brought to by abject servitude, poverty, ignorance, and vice" (qtd. in Burke's Report 386), and who threatened to blight "the morals, principles, stability, and character of the nation itself" (qtd. in Burke's Report 388). Hazard had little patience for the abstract idealism of his opponents, and his cutting words left little room for interpretation; the ruling elite was not interested in relinquishing power.

Feeding on anti-Catholic sentiments, the opponents of reform also made use of widespread xenophobia to justify the state's political inequality. For many of the state's residents, restrictions on voting rights were a worthwhile price to pay as long as it ensured that the state's Catholic population remained underrepresented.[15] The following excerpt published in the conservative *Providence Journal* summarizes some of the most base, but persistent, anti-Catholic sentiments that prevailed at the time:

> They [Catholics] will league and band together and usurp our native political power. Their priests and leaders will say to a political party as they say in New York City, give us by law every opportunity to perpetuate our spiritual despotism. At the feet of these men will you lay down your freedom. Foreigners still remain foreign and are still embraced by mother church. He still bows down to her rituals, worships the host, and obeys and craves absolution from the priest. He cannot be assimilated. Now is the time to choose between two systems—the conservative checks or foreigners only responsible to priests. (*Providence Journal,* March 19, 1842, reprinted in Conley 319–323.)

Other conservatives chose not to defend the inequalities that arose through the existing system, but instead defended the Charter Government by stressing the importance of rule of law and of achieving political reform through the existing political institutions. For them the choice was not between popular sovereignty and tyranny, as the reformers declared, the choice was between law and order and political anarchy.[16]

To address political ills through extra-legal means was a cure worse than the disease. It threatened the very foundation of civil authority—the sanctity of laws. To allow the insurgents to succeed in their radical plan was intolerable to the Charter supporters, even among the moderates. The law and order side asserted that in the absence of substantial societal grievances or insurmountable political ills, there was no legitimate justification for pursuing reform through extra-legal means, and absolutely no justification for pursuing reform through the threat of force (Pitman, "A Reply" 20–21).

The Charterites developed a fluid political strategy, designed to match each move by Dorr's side. The initial strategy was simply to ignore the reformers and the larger reform fervor that swept the state. The conservatives recalled that previous cries for reform had burned bright for short periods of time, only to fade quickly. They anticipated that the latest round of unpleasantness would also pass with time.

When this strategy failed to defuse the situation, the conservatives offered a series of belated compromises, each of which came too late and offered too little to satisfy the emboldened reformers. The Charter side used compromise, like a professional boxer uses foot movement, not so much to retreat, but to reposition itself for strategic advantage. Each "compromise" was designed to draw moderates away from the suffragists' cause and to delay substantive reform. But as the promise of compromise typically came shortly after an impressive show of strength by the reform side, it was offered at a time when it was least likely to be accepted.

After Dorr's side produced the People's Constitution in November of 1841 and ratified their Constitution in a one-sided referendum in December, the Charter side returned to the table—continuing the cycle of reform success followed by reluctant appeasement by the Charter supporters. In January of 1842, the Charter side completed their own draft constitution, referred to as the Landholders' Constitution.

Although late in coming, the Landholders' Constitution addressed some of the flaws associated with the system (Gettleman 61). It called for a more equitable distribution of representation in the Assembly, though it still overrepresented southern agricultural interests, and it eliminated the property requirement for the state's native, white male population. The landholders, appealing to anti-Irish sentiments, kept the property requirement for naturalized citizens and increased the residency requirement for voting from one to three years.[17] Like the People's Constitution, the Landholders' Constitution failed to grant voting rights to the state's African American citizens and made no mention of women's voting rights.

In a world governed by reason, the conflict might have ended shortly after this point.[18] Reform, either in the shape of the People's Constitution or the Landholders' Constitution, was coming to Rhode Island in the spring of 1842. The antiquated Charter would soon be replaced with a modern constitution, the problem of malapportionment would be addressed, and suffrage would be expanded. While the differences between the rival constitutions were real, they were relatively minor when compared to the existing Charter and for most Rhode Islanders not worth the horror associated with civil war.

But to the dismay of moderates on both sides of the issue, the proposed Landholders' Constitution did not resolve the situation, as it was rejected by a popular referendum in late March of 1842.[19] Hard-line conservatives, who opposed any disruption to the existing political order, joined forces with steadfast reformers, who saw no need for the proposed constitution since the People's Constitution had already been ratified. The unholy alliance defeated the Landholders' Constitution by a margin of less than seven hundred votes, putting to rest the best chance to resolve the conflict through political, rather than forceful, means.

With the hope of an electoral solution dashed, the Charter side prepared to defend the established order by force. The General Assembly convened in a special session to prepare for the conflict that now seemed inevitable. On April 7, 1842, just weeks before the scheduled elections to fill the People's Government, the Charter Assembly passed legislation titled "An Act in Relation to Offenses against the Sovereign Power of the State."[20] The law, commonly referred to as the Algerine Law, made it a criminal offense, punishable with a maximum fine of $1,000 and six months in prison, to "receive, record, or certify votes" in the upcoming election. The punishment for allowing one's name to appear as a candidate for the People's Government carried a maximum fine of $2,000 and imprisonment of one year. And for those who dared to exercise power under the People's Constitution, the offense was deemed treason and carried the penalty of life in prison. The law was enacted by the Assembly by a vote of 60 to 6 (Mowry, *The Dorr War* 134).

The Charter side also attempted to strengthen its position by summoning the state's armed militias. The Charter authorities distributed arms to their supporters in Providence, where they were able to fill three armed companies (The First Light Infantry, The Cadets, and Marine Artillery). While additional companies were filled in the towns of Newport, Bristol, and Warren (Hodges 182), Governor King soon found that the state militias were divided in their loyalty (Mowry, *The Dorr War* 140–141). Entire militia units in the northern part of the state and at least two in Providence (United Volunteers and United Train of Artillery) were committed to defend Dorr and his government, while other militias remained uncommitted (Mowry, *The Dorr War* 178). Without sufficient military support under his control, Governor King sent urgent requests to the president for federal intervention.

In Search of Support

As federal assistance now seemed to be the key to success, both sides sent letters and delegations to Washington in search of support.[21] Dorr's delegation, led by Dr. Brown, the President of the Rhode Island Suffrage Association, believed that Article 4, Section 4 of the U.S. Constitution, which guarantees each state "a republican form of government," justified federal support for their side. At the very least, the reformers insisted the federal government allow the state to work out its own internal issue. The law and order delegation, comprised of three prominent members of the Charter Government, argued that the very same clause of the Constitution, which goes on to pledge protection to each state "against domestic violence" and "invasion," required the federal government to support their side. Both delegations left their meetings with President Tyler confident that they had won his support.

The future of the state's electoral process lay in the hands of the president, an ironic situation since Tyler had risen to the presidency after William Harrison died in office on April 4, 1841, giving Tyler the distinction of being the first American president to obtain the office without an electoral mandate. Tyler's many detractors referred to him as "his ascendancy" and described him as "the acting president," rather than president (Gettleman 95). Tyler was further wounded by the abandonment of his own party, the Whig Party, after he vetoed a series of banking and trade measures supported by congressional Whigs.

Rather than a partisan, Tyler was a Virginian who viewed all issues through the warped lens of slavery. He could not help but fear what the precedent of a populist rebellion would mean for the South. The issue was further complicated by the fact that Rhode Island, with its severely limited voting base, had favored Harrison and Tyler in the 1840 presidential election.[22] If Tyler was going to win the presidency in 1844, something he still believed was possible in the spring of 1842, he would need the support of the Ocean State, which would be unlikely should the state reform its electoral process and dramatically increase its percentage of working-class voters.

Following Dr. Brown's meeting with the president, Dorr's men remained confident that the chief executive would not interfere in what they considered a state affair. Dr. Brown reported to Dorr that "I have just returned from a visit to the President, and one thing is certain, the President and the Cabinet will never send an armed force to Rhode Island, or in any other way attempt to prevent the people from obtaining and enjoying their just rights" (qtd. in McDougall 220).

On April 11, 1842, one week prior to the scheduled election of the new government under the People's Constitution, President Tyler shocked Dr. Brown and the other suffragists by granting Governor King the ultimate instrument of intimidation, a letter pledging federal support. Tyler wrote that "should the time arrive (and my fervent prayer is that it may never come) when an insurrection shall exist against the government of Rhode Island, and a requisition shall be made upon the Executive of the United States to furnish that protection . . . I shall not be found to shrink from the performance of a duty" (qtd. in Burke's Report 659). With the stroke of a pen, President Tyler had taken sides in the dispute, a fact that was reprinted in the press and widely distributed throughout the state.[23]

While the Algerine Laws, combined with the President's threatening letter, undoubtedly suppressed turnout in the April election,[24] the election for the People's Government went forward without incident. The election was held on April 18, 1842, with Thomas Dorr chosen as the People's Governor, forcing President Tyler to make good on his earlier threats.

On April 25, 1842, Colonel Fanning, in command of U.S. troops at Fort Monroe, Virginia, was ordered to fill two companies and to report to New York Harbor, within striking distance of the quickly escalating Rhode Island conflict. One day later the War Department ordered Colonel Bankhead, the commanding officer of U.S. forces at Fort Columbus, New York, to fill two additional companies and to prepare for "detached service" (Burke's Report 55). Colonel Bankhead and the two artillery companies arrived at Fort Adams in Newport, Rhode Island, on May 2, 1842, one day prior to the scheduled inauguration of Thomas Dorr and his government.

In defiance of the Charter government and the Federal government, Thomas Dorr was sworn in as the state's first constitutionally elected governor on May 3, 1842. To the Charter Government, the candidates who dared run for office under the People's Constitution were now outlaws; to the thousands of people who voted for the People's Government, the newly elected officials were nothing less than heroes. To them, the new government and the constitution on which it was founded had reestablished the sacred covenant of democracy and was cause for celebration.

Following the inauguration, Dorr hoped to march with his armed supporters, nearly a thousand strong, and seize control of the government. Dorr later recalled the missed opportunity, "The tide was at the flood . . . The numerous array of our brethren in arms on the occasion of the inauguration . . . were both prepared and desirous to maintain the government of their choice" (qtd. in Burke's Report 738). Dorr's impulse to take possession of the physical controls of government was checked by moderates within the newly founded People's Legislature. Moderate reformers within the People's Assembly insisted that a delegation travel to Washington to consult with federal authorities, an idea Dorr opposed, as he believed that the federal government had no role to play in this internal state issue.[25] Dorr argued that any further delay would only strengthen his political enemies and would most certainly prove futile, as President Tyler had already taken sides in the conflict.

In the end, Dorr stayed true to his principles and abided by the will of the legislature, explaining that as the People's Governor it was not his function "to make the laws or to direct the lawmakers, but to execute their acts and orders" (qtd. in Burke's Report 739). While in Washington, Dorr met with President Tyler and members of Congress, only to have his fears confirmed. Not only would the President not support Dorr's government, but in the event that violence should erupt in Rhode Island, the President confirmed that federal troops would be made available to assist the Charter Government (Mowry, "Tammany Hall" 295).

Governor Dorr's trip to Washington, however, proved important in ways that no one had anticipated. On his return journey, the disheartened Dorr made a brief stop in New York, where he was given a hero's welcome by the leading figures of Tammany Hall (Mowry, *The Dorr War* 171–173). Dorr's New York excursion

ended with a parade in which an estimated five hundred supporters, accompanied by a band and a company of volunteer firemen,
encouraged Dorr to continue Rhode Island's constitutional struggle. The highlight of Dorr's New York visit came in the form of a
letter, co-authored by Alexander Ming (Col. 13 Reg't. N.Y.A) and
Abraham Crasto (Lt. Col. 236 Reg't. N.Y. S. I.). In this letter, two
of the state's leading militia leaders notified Dorr that "several military companies" had offered "their services to form a military escort to accompany" Dorr back to his home state of Rhode Island
(Mowry, "Tammany Hall" 296). Another New Yorker, Levi D.
Slamm, informed Dorr that he had chartered a steamboat to carry
a thousand armed supporters to Rhode Island should a conflict
erupt (Schlesinger 411–413). These pledges of support were added
to commitments Dorr had already received from Louis Lapham
(an abolitionist from Massachusetts who pledged the backing of
three hundred armed supporters (Dennison 74), and from other
militia leaders in Pennsylvania (Dennison 81).

Meanwhile, back in Rhode Island, Governor King convened
a war council in the chambers of the old market house in Providence to advise him during the conflict (Mowry 147 and Dyer
14). Police companies were filled and the Riot Act was amended
to permit military force without delay (Dennison 77). The Charter
Assembly declared the presence of outright insurrection in the
state and began arresting members of the People's Government.
Dorr would soon return to Rhode Island, with armed supporters
within his state sworn to protect him, as well as armed supporters
from other states ready to enter the contest if called. The nation
was faced with an irreconcilable conflict and no acceptable mechanism to resolve it—civil war seemed inevitable.

Words to Deeds

Upon his arrival in Providence, Dorr was treated to a hero's
welcome, with roughly three thousand supporters turning out to

greet him. An impromptu parade of twelve hundred followers, a fourth of whom were armed, formed a procession[26] that snaked through the city's streets for more than two hours. The line of working-class citizens included one hundred members of organized militias, seventy-five men on horseback, and a boisterous marching band. At the head of the line was Governor Dorr, carrying a sword and riding in an open-air coach—a barouche—pulled by a team of four white horses (Mowry, *Dorr War* 175; and Frieze 83).

Dorr's parade concluded at the home of Burrington Anthony, the former federal marshal elected as the Sheriff of Providence under the People's Government. It was here, after hours of travel and covered in dust that Dorr stood in his raised carriage and delivered an impassioned forty-five minute speech. One Charter supporter recalled Dorr appearing as "one of the most fierce looking men I ever saw" (qtd. in Pitman, *Report on the Trial* 28). While an exact transcript of the speech has not survived, most accounts recall Dorr reiterating his now common themes.

The speech restated the case that legitimate governmental authority is derived from the consent of the governed and that the majority of the state's population had chosen to replace the Charter Government with the democratically elected People's Government. He restated the ills suffered under the old regime, including malapportionment and limited suffrage. He condemned the Charter authorities for enacting their restrictive laws and for resisting the will of the people with the threat of force. He asserted that the supporters of suffrage existed in large numbers throughout the Union and were amassing in places like New York and Pennsylvania to assist the Rhode Island reformers. He explicitly stated that he had been promised five thousand men from New York.[27] Should the hired forces of the general government enter the fray, he promised, "the contest will then become national and our State the battleground of American freedom" (Burke's Report 679–680).[28] At one point he raised a sword in the air, a sword that had been given to him by supporters in New York, and pronounced that it had been "dipped in blood once, and rather than yield the rights of the people of Rhode Island, it should be buried in gore to its hilt" (William Blodget's testimony in Pitman, *Report on the Trial* 27). Dorr was preparing the crowd, and perhaps himself, for the battle to come. The speech served as the bridge from words to deeds. Peaceful means for resolving this irreconcilable conflict had been exhausted. For those who lacked the desire or will for armed struggle, the time had come to depart the cause; for those willing to fight for political rights, it was now time to take up arms in the defense of liberty.

But instead of launching an immediate attack, Dorr and his advisors assembled to determine their strategy. Together with his military leaders, Dorr hatched a simple plan; the suffragists would attack the arsenal and then establish a military base on the campus of Brown College in the heart of Providence (Mowry, *The Dorr War* 182; Hodges 185). The arms from the arsenal and fortified buildings of the college would provide the suffragists ample protection from the Charter side. From there, Dorr's men would take possession of the state's public buildings, which they believed rightfully belonged under the control of the People's Government. Should the federal government defend the Charter side, the Dorrites would have sufficient protection and arms to withstand the initial attack and soon reinforcements would arrive from New York and elsewhere.

The Dorrites were convinced that behind the arsenal's stone walls rested the key to their success. The building was situated in an open field referred to as the Dexter Train Grounds. The site was named in honor of Ebenezer Knight Dexter who donated the twenty-acre parcel to the city for the purpose of militia training (Hodges 182). The arsenal stood fifty-by-sixty feet and was two stories tall. Its walls were made of chip stone, twenty-eight inches thick at the base and narrowing to eighteen inches at the structure's highest point. It contained twenty-eight windows from which to fire its cannons and muskets and only two doors for entry (Scott; Dyer 28–29).

Five cannons[29] loaded with grape and canister were positioned by the Charter side near the arsenal's doors and lower windows (Leonard Blodget qtd. in Pitman, *Report on the Trial* 39). The choice of projectile was chosen for its broad and lethal impact. Rather than make use of standard cannon balls, which could provide a focused punch, the use of grape and canister enabled the Charter forces to deliver a deadly spray of shrapnel across a wide field of battle. The Charter force used the same logic when loading their rifles with duck shot. One defender explained, "The most effective missiles appeared to be the coarsest kind of duck shot, preferably to single bullets, for wider distribution on a crowd" (Allen). Since the arsenal was positioned in an open field that provided virtually no cover for Dorr's side, the use of grape and duck shot promised to provide maximum effect.

Upon arrival at the arsenal, Dorr initially positioned his cannons at a distance of about two hundred yards from the building, surrounded by a small stand of trees (Hodges 187). True to form, Dorr announced the presence of his troops not by cannon fire, but by a formal declaration. An officer in Dorr's force was instructed to approach the arsenal under the white flag of truce. With a white handkerchief attached to his sword, Dorr's officer knocked on the arsenal's iron door and delivered a message to commanding officer of the Charter side. Dorr's officer demanded that the Charter forces surrender the arsenal to Governor Dorr, to which the commanding officer of the Charter side responded that if Dorr wanted the arsenal he should "come and take it" (William Blodget's testimony in Pitman, *Report on the Trial* 38).

Faced with the brazen response, Dorr's supporters were forced to choose between two unpleasant responses—fight or flight. The notion that the Charter side would peacefully cede power when confronted with Dorr's force, as had been widely predicted by the suffragists, proved false. The insurgents would either retreat in disgrace or they would attack. Dorr's commanding officer, Col. Wheeler, and a majority of the men that Col. Wheeler commanded, chose to retreat. Colonel Dispeau and the Pawtucket Company that he commanded also retreated (Charles W. Carter's testimony in Pitman, *Report on the Trial* 69; Burke's Report 906–907). Dorr, on the other hand, chose to defy the odds and attack. Governor Dorr took control of the remaining troops and reestablished order. With his remaining force, Dorr moved forward with the plan. His two cannons were leveled directly at the stone structure. A torch was raised, the order was given to fire the first cannon, and the cannon flashed, but failed to discharge. The order was given to fire the second cannon; it too flashed, but failed to fire. Dorr proclaimed, "I am betrayed," as he and his men, now fully exposed to the Charter force, had no choice but to retreat from the field.[30]

No one knows with certainty why the cannons failed. A leading theory suggests that a Judas figure, Hiram Chappell, betrayed Dorr by plugging the cannons and causing them to misfire. All that is known about Chappell is that he served as an escort to Dorr during his triumphant return to Providence on May 16, and that on the 17th of May, Chappell was instructed to purchase four or five kegs of powder with twenty-five dollars worth of gold quarter eagles given to him by Dorr (Pitman, *Report on the Trial* 34). When questioned by the Charter Commissioners following the failed attack, Chappell reported that he plugged the bronze cannons; later, while being harassed in prison by Dorr's supporters, Chappell recanted and denied plugging the guns (Pitman, *Report on the Trial.* 48; Burke's Report 893). Two years after the failed attack, no longer fearing arrest from the Charter authorities or threat from Dorr's supporters, Chappell once again reported plugging the guns.[31]

But ultimately it matters little why the cannons failed. In reality, the fight was lost prior to the order to fire. Dorr, profoundly disappointed with the night's events, recalled that "the people were called, and they did not come" and those who did arrive did not stay very long. He went on to say, "the people as a body, let it be said, were unwilling, or unable; they were deterred by the threats of the President, or debarred by the mailed hand of a military despotism. Be it as it may, they did not come" (Burke's Report 757).

For a man who drew his strength from the support of the masses, the abandonment was almost more than he could stand. He concluded in despair that "it was our friends, and not our enemies, who conquered us" (Burke's Report 758).

Dorr was forced to acknowledge what he had failed to see until that point; he had lost the will of the people during his struggle to gain control of the government. Hiram Chappell, on the other hand, who had waited with Dorr on the night of the attack for the reinforcements who failed to arrived, who had been at the headquarters as Dorr's own father pleaded with him against the use of force, and who was on the field when Dorr's officers fled, must have seen through the fog of war. Chappell certainly realized that to take military action against the state and federal government without overwhelming popular support was madness. Not only would the plan fail and would lives be lost, it would do nothing to promote the electoral reforms that were so near. Chappell's act of disobedience, if in fact he plugged the cannons, would not have been an act of betrayal, it would have been an act of mercy.

As news of the quixotic attack reached New York, support for Dorr's military effort, which only hours before had reached its pinnacle, melted in an instant (*National Intelligencer,* May 24, 1842; and Mowry, *The Dorr War* 194–195). The New York supporters had promised to assist the suffragists when faced with federal troops. But if the Rhode Island suffragists lacked the will to defeat the state's Charter forces, as it now appeared, support from New York was futile. Just as New Yorkers would not tolerate the federal government imposing its will on Rhode Island, New Yorkers would not impose their preference on their reluctant neighbors to the north.

The Aftermath

The annals of history are strewn with tales of men willing to kill and die in the heat of passion. Far fewer are willing to do the same in the cold pursuit of a just cause, and fewer yet for a cause that promises no personal gain. The rarest of all, perhaps for good reason, are those willing to lead such an effort when opposed by the full force of an established authority, respected friends, and close relatives. Such was the case for Thomas Wilson Dorr, making him either a hero or a fool depending on one's perspective.

The suffragist leaders, increasingly isolated and marginalized, remained confident in the righteousness of their cause and the inevitability of their success. The reformers would learn firsthand that the macro-level narrative of democracy, which often makes the spread of democracy appear inevitable, is far different than the micro-level narrative that reveals an unpredictable struggle carried out by each generation. The reformers also underestimated the strength of the Charter resistance, ignoring one of the few truisms in politics—that there is nothing more dangerous and unpredictable than a cabal of grey-haired men with titles fighting for their political survival.

Dorr's final error in judgment was in overestimating the willingness of the suffragists to use force. Blinded by principle, Dorr never fully understood why his support grew weaker as the crisis reached its pinnacle. Many moderate reformers simply rejected the use of force. It was not that they necessarily adhered to lower principles or held weaker convictions, as Dorr lamented. If the price of a total victory, victory without compromise, was the shedding of blood, many of the moderates were content to settle for a less definitive outcome. For them, the threatening rhetoric of their campaign was just that, words to be used as a catalyst for change—and if change was to come slowly and incrementally, but peacefully, so be it. They were confident that the momentum of history was moving in their direction, making patience a virtue, not a weakness.

The Charter side made mistakes of their own. They were clearly emboldened by the promise of federal support and the strength of their military position. In their resistance to change, they ignored another political truism—the river of democracy grows wider and stronger as it flows toward its source (the people), eventually eroding away all barriers. Stated differently, political systems based on the precept of popular sovereignty tend to become more democratic, not less, over time. The conservatives underestimated the reform movement, believing it to be another fleeting cause that might burn bright for a moment, but that would soon return to a controllable smolder. Finding themselves on the wrong side of history, they undertook a strategy of delay, deception, and intimidation. Their rigidity fomented the radical element of the reform movement and threatened the social order the conservatives held dear.

In June, the Charter side easily put down Dorr's second and final attempt at exercising military power, a desperate attempt to assemble supporters in the village of Chepachet. Like the failed arsenal attack, the Chepachet episode ended without a direct confrontation, as Dorr wisely dismissed his disappointingly small band of armed supporters when faced with overwhelming opposition. The Charter side continued their show of force by declaring martial law, arresting suspected Dorr supporters, and causing Dorr to flee the state. When Dorr eventually returned to Providence, he was promptly arrested and sentenced to spend the remainder of his life in solitary confinement.

The Charter side would eventually learn that its military campaign, while successful in the short run, could not derail the democratic reform movement. Despite its military prowess, the Charter side lost the political battle. In November of 1842, the state's voters approved a new constitution, dubbed the Algerine Constitution by the more extreme Dorrites who opposed it in principle. The new governing document addressed the malapportionment issue and replaced the landowning requirement for native residence with a less burdensome $1 poll tax. Naturalized citizens, however, were still barred from the polls unless they lived in the state for at least two years and owned $134 in property. With ratification of the constitution, the moderate suffragists had won a small victory and would eventually win others, including the expansion of voting rights for the state's African American residents.

Dorr, while in prison, proved far more powerful as a martyr than he had as a military commander. A politically active liberation society quickly formed to agitate for his release. The liberation society successfully made Dorr's release a political issue, forcing candidates to either pledge their support for Dorr's liberation, or to be held accountable by the electorate. Fearing the political fallout from the growing liberation movement, the Assembly agreed to release Dorr if he pledged allegiance to the state. Having risked everything for principle, Dorr refused anything but an unconditional release, which he was granted by the Assembly in June of 1845, after spending twenty months in prison. In 1851 the Assembly, now controlled by pro-Dorr Democrats, voted to restore Dorr's political rights and shortly afterwards annulled his treason conviction.

When Dorr died in 1854, the state was governed by a constitution, suffrage had been expanded, the problem of malapportionment had been meaningfully addressed, and Dorr's name had been cleared of all wrongdoing. Dorr died at the age of forty-nine, physically broken from his time in prison, but with his principles intact. His small disturbance had successfully shaken the state out of its political slumber and moved the country a step forward on its journey toward democratic governance.

Notes

1. Portions of this essay are reprinted with permission from Howard R. Ernst's "A Call to Arms: Thomas Wilson Dorr's Forceful Effort to Implement the People's Constitution." *Rhode Island History*. Rhode Island Historical Society, Fall 2008.
2. For a complete account of the attack on the arsenal see Ernst 2008. For differing reports on the size of the insurgent groups see: Mowry, *The Dorr War* 184; McDougall 244; and testimony of Charles W. Carter, in Pitman, *Report on the Trial* 68. Though smaller than Dorr desired, his force was still considerably larger than the Charter force in the arsenal. Edward H. Hazard, who was in the arsenal, reported that the

defenders numbered 160 men (Testimony of Edward H. Hazard, in Pitman, *Report on the Trial* 29).

3. For an excellent discussion of Dorr's experience at Harvard see Gettleman 13–15.

4. For comparisons of Rhode Island's reform movement to those in other states see Hartz; McMaster; and Williamson.

5. By the early 19th century Rhode Island was not alone in requiring the ownership of property as a qualification for political participation. An 1829 report written by Benjamin Hazard, a staunch supporter of the property requirement, found that of the twenty-four states in the Union at the time, only seven were free from all forms of property qualification (Maine, Vermont, Kentucky, Illinois, Alabama, Indiana, and Missouri); seven other states required the payment of taxes as evidence of property (New Hampshire, Massachusetts, Pennsylvania, Delaware, Ohio, Georgia, and Louisiana); two states permitted service in the militia to substitute for the payment of taxes (New York and Mississippi), and eight states possessed a significant property requirement (Rhode Island, Virginia, Connecticut, Maryland, North Carolina, South Carolina, Tennessee, and New Jersey).

6. See Benjamin Hazard's 1829 "Report on the Extension of Suffrage," reprinted in Burke's Report (U.S. Congress, House), *Interference of the Executive in the Affairs of Rhode Island,* Report No. 546, 28 Congress, 1 Session, 1884, pg. 385.

7. Note that owning a sizable estate was not a guarantee of political rights. Political participation still required the approval of the existing freemen in a particular town. While there is some evidence that not all property owners were granted the status of freemen, the evidence does not suggest that this practice was widespread by the 19th century. For more on this, see Burke's Report 10.

8. Rhode Island's total population in 1840 is estimated to have been 108,837, with 9,590 eligible voters. See Burke's Report 11; Conley 296; and King 26–27.

9. For discussions of early efforts to adopt a state constitution see, Burke's Report 14–15; Gettleman 23–29; Dennison 14–15, and 18; King 28–29; and Mowry, *The Dorr War* 28–38.

10. Mowry, *The Dorr War* 50 mistakenly reports that the Association was formed in the autumn of 1840. It is likely that Mowry relied on an error in Burke's Report 16. Conley 294; Gettleman 34; and Dennison 36 correctly report that the association was formed in the spring of 1840. Confusion regarding the formation of the Suffrage Association probably relates to the fact that the group became more active in the fall of 1840 (see Dennison 36).

11. For a description of the suffragists during the mid-1830s, see Gettleman 22–23.

12. This passage concluded the association's charter and served as its rallying call (Dennison 36).

13. For a description of the Dillingham Petition see Conley 300.

14. For a discussion of the many resolutions passed by the reformers, see King ch. 3.

15. For an excellent treatment of the role of nativism in the suffrage movement, see Conley 319–322.

16. It is interesting to note that while the Charter supporters shared Madison's preference for representative democracy over more direct forms of democracy, Madison and the nation's founders were far less concerned with following established legal mechanisms than the Rhode Island Charter supporters. In fact, the delegates at the

Philadelphia Convention who drafted the U.S. Constitution rejected the established legal mechanisms of the day. Congress had explicitly restricted the authority of the delegates by stating that the delegates at the Philadelphia Convention should meet:

> For the sole and expressed purpose of revising the Articles of Confederation and reporting to Congress and the several legislatures such alterations and provisions therein as shall, when agreed to in Congress and confirmed by the states, render the federal constitution adequate to the exigencies of Government & the preservation of the Union.

Instead, the delegates drafted an entirely new Constitution, submitted their unauthorized Constitution to special ratification conventions within each state, and called for the Constitution to go into effect after being approved by only three-fourths of the states, rejecting the requirement for unanimity specified by the Articles of Confederation. Like the nation's Founders, the reformers had decided to take their case directly to the sovereign people, and in doing so, ignored the established law.

17. For a comparison of the two constitutions see, Conley 320; and Mowry, *The Dorr War* 101–104.
18. For an argument that accuses the leaders of the reform movement of ideological extremism and obstructing a peaceful resolution to the crisis, see Dennison 61.
19. For more on the election process, see King ch. 4.
20. For a draft of the legislation see King ch. 5. For a discussion of the law see Burke's Report 65–69.
21. The reformers and the Charter side sent delegations in April and May of 1842.
22. The presidential vote in Rhode Island was 5,278 for Harrison and to 3,301 for Van Buren (Conley 298).
23. The letter was reprinted in the *Providence Daily Journal* on April 15, 1842.
24. Voter turnout declined from the constitutional election (December 1841) and the candidate election (April 1842) by 2,330 votes.
25. See Dorr's 1843 "Address to the People of Rhode Island," reprinted in Burke's Report 738 and Dennison 50–51.
26. There are numerous conflicting reports regarding the size and nature of Dorr's welcome party in Providence. The actual number of supporters was likely somewhere between 1,200 and 3,000, while the number of men under arms remains less clear. The numbers cited in this section are from Mowry, *The Dorr War* 175–176. Mowry's work provides the most detailed account of the events and is likely the most accurate. For other accounts see Jewett 3; and Pitman, *Report on the Trial*.
27. For an excellent analysis of various interpretations of Dorr's sword speech, see Mowry, *The Dorr War* 176–177.
28. For conflicting accounts of Dorr's speech see Burke's Report 679–680; Dennison 84; and Hodges 183.
29. It is unclear the size of the cannons. One report claims they were large guns, ranging in size from 12 to 48-pounders (see Hodges 182). Col. Blodget reports they were far smaller of six-pound caliber (see testimony of Leonard Blodget, printed in Pitman, *Report on the Trial* 39).
30. For accounts of Dorr's reaction see testimony of William P. Blodget in Pitman, *Report on the Trial*. 27 and 38; McDougall 244.
31. For more on this topic see Testimony of Hiram Chappell qtd. in Pitman, *Report on the Trial* 37; Burke's Report 882.

References

Allen, Zachariah. "The Dorr War: Mr. Zachariah Allen Relates the Events of May 17 and 18, 1842." *The Providence Press,* Supplement, May 7, 1881.

Burke's Report (U.S. Congress, House), *Interference of the Executive in the Affairs of Rhode Island,* Report No. 546, 28 Congress, 1 Session, 1884.

Congdon, Charles T. *Reminiscences of a Journalist.* Boston: James R. Osgood and Company, 1880.

Conley, Patrick T. *Democracy in Decline: Rhode Island's Constitutional Period, 1776– 1841.* Providence, RI: Rhode Island Historical Society, 1977.

Dennison, George M. *The Dorr War: Republicanism on Trial, 1831–1861.* Lexington, KY: The University Press of Kentucky, 1976.

Dyer, Elisha. *Reminiscences of Rhode Island in 1842: As Connected with the Dorr Rebellion.* Providence: self-published, 1888.

Ernst, Howard R. "A Call to Arms: Thomas Wilson Dorr's Forceful Effort to Implement the People's Constitution." *Rhode Island History.* Rhode Island Historical Society, Fall 2008.

Frieze, Jacob. *Concise History of the Efforts to Obtain an Extension of Suffrage in Rhode Island.* Providence, RI: Benjamin F. Moore Printer, 1842.

Gettleman, Marvin E. *The Dorr Rebellion: A Study in American Radicalism, 1833–1849.* New York: Random House, 1973 (reprinted New York: Robert E. Krieger Publishing Co., 1980).

Hartz, Louis. *The Liberal Tradition in America: An Interpretation of American Political Thought since the Revolution.* New York: Harcourt, Brace & World, 1955.

Hodges, Almon Danforth. *Almon Danforth Hodges and His Neighbors: An Autobiographical Sketch of a Typical Old New Englander.* Boston: Privately Printed, 1909.

Jewett, Charles Coffin. *The Close of the Late Rebellion in Rhode Island.* Providence, RI: B. Cranston & Co., 1842.

King, Dan. *The Life and Times of Thomas Wilson Dorr.* Boston: published by the author, 1859 (reprinted Freeport, NY: Books for Library Press, 1969).

Madison, James. *Notes of Debates in the Federal Convention of 1787.* New York: W.W. Norton & Company, 1987.

McDougall, Francis H. *Might and Right.* Providence, RI: A.H. Stillwell, 1844.

McMaster, John Bach. *The Acquisition of Political, Social, and Industrial Rights of Man in America.* Cleveland: Imperial Press, 1903.

Morison, Samuel Eliot. "The Great Rebellion in Harvard College and the Resignation of President Kirkland." *Transactions of the Colonial Society of Massachusetts, 1927– 1928.* Boston: The Society, 1929.

Morison, Samuel Eliot. *Three Centuries of Harvard, 1636–1936.* Cambridge, Mass: Harvard University Press, 1936.

Mowry, Arthur May. "Tammany Hall and the Dorr Rebellion." *The American Historical Review* 3 (January 1898): 292–301.

Mowry, Arthur May. *The Dorr War, or the Constitutional Struggle in Rhode Island.* Providence, RI: Preston & Rounds Company, 1901 (reprinted NY: Johnson Reprint Corporation, 1968).

Pitman, John. *A Reply to the Letter of the Hon. Marcus Morton, Late Governor of Massachusetts Regarding the Rhode Island Question.* Providence: Knowles and Vose, 1842.

Pitman, Joseph S. *Report on the Trial of Thomas Wilson Dorr for Treason.* Boston: Tappan & Dennet, 1844.

Schlesinger, Arthur M., Jr. *The Age of Jackson.* Boston: Little, Brown and Company, 1946.

Scott, Winfield Townley. *Sword on the Table: Thomas Dorr's Rebellion.* Norfolk, Connecticut: New Directions, 1942.

Williamson, Chilton. *American Suffrage: From Property to Democracy, 1760–1860.* Princeton, NJ: Princeton University Press, 1960.

Questions

1. Looking back in history, it could be argued that this rebellion marked one of the final chapters in America's "revolutionary period," more accurately the epilogue of the American Revolution. No longer *the* central principle upon which all legitimate governmental authority was derived, popular sovereignty survived the period reduced in stature. In its "post-revolutionary" period how has the meaning of popular sovereignty changed?

2. Looking forward from the rebellion, we see that it marked an important beginning for America. It was a vital first step in the nation's long struggle to win civil rights for its disenfranchised majority. While civil disobedience and mass protest have replaced rebellion as the preferred instruments of change, the struggle for civil rights continues. What are the lessons of the Dorr War for those who continue to struggle for full political participation in the political process?

3. In the post-9/11 world, in which the federal government has asserted vast powers in the name of national security, the natural tension between security and liberty, which defined the Dorr conflict, has become a defining theme of the current context. Apply the lessons of the Dorr conflict to the nation's current struggle to balance the need to protect civil liberties with the desire for national security?

4. This case suggests that many of the Founders were not nearly as democratically-minded as is often assumed. It reveals that the conflict that arose in Rhode Island was not a repudiation of the Founding ideals or the unintended consequence of a constitutional flaw—it was an extension of a key founding debate regarding who in society should be permitted to vote. Making use of the arguments put forth by the proponents and opponents of expanded suffrage rights during the Dorr War, consider the merits of

granting voting rights to sixteen year olds, to convicted felons who have
served their time, or to undocumented immigrants?

5.   A theme of this essay is American federalism, the relationship between
the federal government and the states. With President Tyler siding with the
Charter Government, a move that upset pro-Dorr supporters throughout
the region, the issue quickly expanded into the realm of states' rights. The
federal government was not only opposing a democratic movement, it was
also meddling in an internal state issue. Suppose for a moment that Dorr's
cannons did fire and his supporters took the arsenal as planned. Is it likely
that federal troops would have been used to suppress Dorr's movement?
Would Dorr's supporters in New York and surrounding states have defended Dorr?

6.   There is little doubt that Thomas Dorr was a highly intelligent young
man who was committed to defending the principles he held dear. While
his opponents saw him as stubborn and headstrong, his supporters viewed
him as dedicated and honorable. Life is never easy for those who are keenly aware of injustice and who have no tolerance for hypocrisy. Does Dorr's
commitment to principle make him a patriot (albeit a tragic one) or does
it making him a lesser character? Are there political principles for which
you would level deadly force against your own family, as Dorr did?

PART TWO

LEGISLATIVE BRANCH

Re-Presentation— The Intricate Dance of Congressional Representation

STEPHEN E. FRANTZICH

No term was mentioned more often in the debate over the U.S. Constitution than "representation" and its variants. Representation is the key link allowing the citizenry to have a say in the complex issues of government. It is one thing to assert the importance of representation, and another to put it into practice. Alternative methods of representation have different theoretical roots and practical implications. Real world applications of representation provide ethical challenges for both elected officials and members of the public. The media often report the actions of Congress as a whole when Congress passes or rejects legislation, but behind the aggregate vote totals are over 500 individual decisions. While most are based on predicable patterns of party or regional support, others generate considerable anxiety, such as when members decide on issues of peace and war. In this chapter we will explore the concept of representation in theory and in practice. The goal is to understand the role of a representative in our democracy.

It was a typical day on the hill. The lights and buzzers on the office clock indicated that postponing the inevitable was no longer possible. A vote was occurring on the House floor and the House member had fifteen minutes to do his ultimate duty, representing the over 650,000 people in his district. He grabbed a stack of constituent letters, waved off his staff, and began his trek from the ornate Rayburn House Office Building to the Capitol across the street.

Former House Speaker, Texan Sam Rayburn (who served as Speaker from 1941–1961, with two breaks when the Republicans controlled the House) would be surprised by many characteristics of the contemporary House. In one sense, House members have become more insulated from political pressure as voter partisanship and the clever drawing of congressional districts have made more members electorally secure. On the other hand, the installation of cameras to cover the House floor proceedings in 1979, new rules opening most committee meetings to outside scrutiny, and the speed of contemporary news coverage on television and the Internet have stripped away much of the anonymity under which earlier members of Congress worked.

Contemporary members are bombarded with advice from colleagues, staff, constituents, interest groups, and spokespersons for the White House or bureaucracy. In reality, members of Congress, like most politicians, are strategically conservative. The prevailing desire to remain in office at virtually any cost (Mayhew) could be interpreted as ego run wild, while members are more likely to point out that one cannot be a statesman out of office. While the probabilities that one vote could threaten their career is very slight, no one wants to be on the wrong side of the odds. Every member of Congress carries around the memory of some former member who lost an election, or almost lost an election, because of a perceived legislative misstep, and he or she harbors the prayer, "Oh, please don't let that be me."

As the House member embarks on the almost four-block walk to the Capitol, he does not mind that he has already made the walk four times that day. It gives him some time to collect his thoughts. While he would love to get out in the sunshine, walking outside would make him a target of the lobbyists. He opts for one of the tunnels, closed to lobbyists and tourists since the terrorist attacks on September 11, 2001. He could speed up the trip on one of the underground subway cars, but he chooses to extend the time alone by walking. He has the route timed down to the second to get to the floor within the last two minutes of the vote. As he takes the elevator up and enters his party's lobby off the chamber, he anticipates running the friendly gauntlet of colleagues lobbying for and against the bill. The lobbies have given their names to paid advocates pushing for legislation. In the past, lobbyists were allowed into these areas and often "buttonholed" members, grabbing their lapels until they could make their pitch. Today colleagues stand around in these rooms trying to garner support. Some have been designated as "whips" by their parties, charged with gathering information on voting intentions and rounding up supportive votes. While most of the attempts to influence votes are cordial and subtle, when the outcome looks close, a great deal of pressure may get unleashed. Threats and promises are not out of the question when the outcome of important legislation is at stake. Members considering voting against their party's position often wait until the last minute to dash to the floor, to have their vote recorded on the electronic vote system.

House members generally vote electronically, placing an ID card in one of many receptacles and voting "yes," "no," or "present." Party leaders monitor ongoing votes and pick out targets for last-minute influence attempts. House votes are generally limited to 15 minutes, limiting the ability to change votes. The situation in the Senate varies along a number of dimensions. Senate constituencies made up of entire states are more heterogeneous, making it more difficult to please a critical mass of voters. On the other hand, the six-year terms of Senators insulates them more from the voters. Voting in the Senate is a much more leisurely process, with oral roll calls votes taking over a half hour, providing more time for negotiations on the floor.

The Founders Take on Representation

Little challenged the Founders more than the concept of representation. In the *Federalist Papers*, which were, in effect, op-ed letters designed to promote the adoption of the Constitution, Alexander Hamilton, James Madison, and John Jay reflected much of the debate at the constitutional convention over representation. *Federalist 63* firmly asserted that "The difference most relied on, between the American and other republics, consists in the principle of representation." "Representation" and its variants ("representative" and "republic") are the most common terms mentioned in the *Federalist Papers.* Much of the Founders' concern during the Constitutional Convention focused on who deserved representation more than how it should be done. Proposals for differing mechanisms came embedded with significant self-interest. Slaveholding states wanted slaves counted for representation but had no intention of granting slaves the power of using that representation. Large population states wanted to link representational power to population while small population states argued that their states had interests separate from those of their residents. In a good political manner, the competing perspectives were settled by compromises, counting slaves as 3/5ths of a person and creating a two-house legislature with the House of Representatives bowing to the wishes of the large population states and the Senate better protecting the interests of small population states.

Not entirely trusting in the public will, the Founders recognized the need to establish structures to temper the passions of the citizenry. They saw how linking elected officials to a defined set of constituents could lead to misguided decisions and opted for relatively large and heterogeneous districts arguing that "It may be suggested, that a people spread over an extensive region cannot, like the crowded inhabitants of a small district, be subject to the infection of violent passions, or to the danger of combining in pursuit of unjust measures" *(Federalist 63)*.

Making a virtue out of political necessity, the authors of the *Federalist Papers* pointed out the value of a two-chamber legislature, whose operations, membership, and political constraints would likely vary. In Madison's famous dictum that "ambition must be made to counteract ambition," *(Federalist 51)* Madison asserted, "The people can never willfully betray their own interests; but they may possibly be betrayed by the representatives of the people; and the danger will be evidently greater where the whole legislative trust is lodged in the hands of one body of men, than where the concurrence of separate and dissimilar bodies is required in every public act" *(Federalist 63)*.

In *Federalist 35,* Hamilton takes on the issue of whether representatives need to be like their constituents demographically. He concludes that the election process is enough to give citizens a voice. In *Federalist 10,* Madison outlines his concern over the danger of factions (interest groups and political parties) which have the potential for distorting representation, while at the same time serving as the primary mechanisms for giving the public a voice. He concludes that the dangers of a few powerful factions can be countered by the encouragement of more competing factions, and that large electoral districts and the separation of governmental powers will help keep them in check.

Despite their extraordinary efforts and creative endeavors, the Founders could do little more than create a structure within which representation would thrive or wither, depending on the behavior of those entrusted with its nurture and upkeep.

Re-presenting in a Democracy

Language can be precise and stimulating or vague and confusing. While we like to call our political system a "democracy," few of our procedures and behaviors strictly deserve that moniker. When social decisions are made in a New England town meeting or through direct votes using initiative or referendum, we have moved toward the democracy end of the continuum between autocracy and democracy. Most of our decisions are made in the context of a small "r" republican form of government. Republics bring the public into the decision-making process indirectly through elections and/or communications with designated representatives. Hannah Pitkin, one of the chief theorists of representation defines it as "acting in the interest of the represented, in a manner responsive to them" (Pitkin, p. 209).

Departing the constitutional convention, senior statesman Benjamin Franklin was asked, "Well, Doctor, what have we got a republic or a monarchy?" "A republic," replied the Doctor, "if you can keep it." The answer clearly outlines the view of a key participant, but also offers a subtle warning that the performance of a political structure is not guaranteed. It depends on the good will, hard work, and intellectual application of a successive set of generations of practitioners.

When the Rubber Hits the Road

"Public office is a public trust." This basic dictate of ethical behavior by elected officials rolls off the tongue with ease, but presents a greater challenge when one attempts to apply it to a real-world situation. Taking bribes, working against the public interest, and other self-serving activities certainly stand out as unethical. In the more mundane and frequent decisions public officials are provided less guidance. It is not clear which public deserves protection and what actually constitutes the best protection. Legislators on all levels of government face these questions every day.

For practical and philosophical reasons, the Founders eschewed pure democracy for a small "r" form of representative government. Candidates would run for office from an identifiable geographic constituency and be expected to represent their interests. The task of the representative would be to re-present, that is, to present a second time, the interests of those who put them in office. Such re-presentation occurs in committee deliberations, conversations with colleagues, and ultimately during one of the thousands of votes on the floor of Congress. Congressional debate and conversation are filled with comments like, "my constituents believe" or "I could never sell that back home." In the grammatically flawed but substantively rich descriptive admonition, legislators are expected to "dance with them that brung you."[1] Members look out for constituents by solving individual problems with the bureaucracy ("casework") and making sure that legislation provides a local benefit.

Debate continues over the degree representatives need to match the demographics of their constituents in order to re-present them effectively. Some argue that unless one has been a farmer— or a woman, minority, union member, and so on—one lacks the substantive understanding and empathy to make their case effectively. On the basis of descriptive representation, Congress fails miserably since it looks very little like the nation in terms of age, gender, race, or prior occupation. In general, Congress is too male (80% versus 49% in the population.), too white (85% versus 75% of the population), too well-educated (almost all have college degrees), too dominated by lawyers (over half of Congress versus less than 1% of the population), and too old (almost twice the average age of the population). While some of these characteristics may help an individual be a better representative (education, occupation, etc.), others are neutral at best. If we were to rely on demographics alone, it would be hard to justify America as a representative democracy. Fortunately, there is an alternative perspective. Re-presentation can be seen as more of a *process* that can be mastered by anyone, whether or not one is like their constituents or not. In this conception, re-representation is a relationship where the representative takes on the responsibility of looking out for the interests of the identifiable members of the population even if the representative does not look like them nor may not agree with them.

The status of "constituent" implies a special relationship between a public official and a subset of the population. Constituents are those who must be "taken into account" in the decision-making process. No elected officials can please everyone all the time. From a practical political perspective elected officials must be able to at least explain their public actions to their constituents.

Serving the public sounds good, but in reality there is often a question of which public and in which way. Issues confronting legislative bodies seldom have one socially and politically correct answer. Legislatures are designed as mediating institutions charged with finding acceptable compromises on issues over which reasonable people disagree. Political preferences usually emerge from values that cannot be proven absolutely right or absolutely wrong. There is no one right social answer to whether we should spend money on national defense or education. No one can factually prove absolutely that a woman's right to choose necessarily trumps the fetus's right to life. While each of us may and should have our own strongly held preference based on what we hold as the ideal world, we have no right to force it on others—except through the political process. The best we can do is to define our preference clearly, marshal existing facts, and attempt to convince others that our preference makes the best social and/or political sense. The politics of the legislative process involves building coalitions behind alternatives with which no one is completely happy, but that a majority can accept. That often results in contradicting the purest form of our own value preferences, but ideally reflects the kind of compromise that retains our loyalty to the political process for the next round of decision-making where our preferences may more effectively prevail. Legislators serve on the front lines of these battles over values.

Individual legislators may serve a constituency with extremely heterogeneous and conflicting views; there are few issues on which the vast majority of their constituents agree. Legislators must determine *who* to represent and *how* do go about doing so.

Most legislators simplify their task by paying exclusive attention to individuals living within their geographically assigned constituencies. Even when they express the desire to represent broader groups, such as all children or all women, they are primarily thinking about the children and women who reside in their district. Most legislators emphasize taking into account those constituents who pay attention to politics, involve themselves in campaigns, and vote. This is not only a wise political strategy, but political activity also serves as a single, short-cut way of determining the degree to which someone is interested in the issue at hand. The assumption is that if a constituent does not care enough to get involved, they have abdicated their right to representation. Representatives usually do not seek problems, but rather wait until a critical mass of constituents bring the issue to their attention.

While the rationale of rewarding active constituents has both practical and political advantages, some ethical questions do arise. How does one deal with individuals legally barred from some or all forms of political involvement (children, legal or illegal aliens, prisoners, etc.) who may well have legitimate claims on the political system? What about individuals lacking the education or skills to get involved? Are they likely to become ignored victims? How does a legislator compensate for the unequal distribution of politically valuable resources? Should wealthy organizations or groups have more say just because they can hire lobbyists and/or make major campaign contributions?

How to Re-Present

A classic conflict in legislative representation revolves around how one should go about re-presenting. Starting from the premise that most constituents lack the time, knowledge, and skill to work out policy compromises, some legislators see themselves as trustees, individuals charged with looking out for the *interests,* but not necessarily the short-term and often poorly thought out *wishes* of constituents. Trustees justify their approach based on their ability to better understand the issues and any long-term implications given their vast experience and ability to focus on politics full time. At best the trustee tries to educate constituents to make their preferences more reasonable and wise. In the legal world, trustees are often provided for children or the mentally challenged, recognizing that they often cannot make wise choices. In the ideal scenario, trustees marshal their knowledge and experience to make compromises with positive long-term implications. The classic statement of the trustee position comes from 18th-century British parliamentarian Edmund Burke, who argued to his constituents:

> Your representative owes you, not his industry only, but his judgment; and he betrays, instead of serving you, if he sacrifices it to your opinion. (Edmund Burke, Speech to the electors of Bristol, 1774)[2]

Deferring to the experience and judgment of an elected official may sound like the appropriate thing to do, but it is not the preference of most voters. Burke felt the sting of his constituents when they withdrew their support and forced him to withdraw his candidacy. The dustbin of political history is filled with legislators misjudging their constituents' preferences or intentionally disregarding them.

John Kennedy's 1955 book, *Profiles in Courage*, written before his presidency, presented a collection of stories of legislators showing the "courage" to act contrary to the wishes of their constituents. In most cases they faced punishment at the polls. While the characterization of courage fits the cases Kennedy chose, since history showed the legislators to be on the right side, it is dangerous to assume that voting against the public will be necessarily a good thing either politically or ethically. One person's courage is another's cowardness, or just plain stupidity. Stubborn legislators, often following their constituents' wishes, have clearly been proven wrong on a number of issues such as segregation and women's rights. Public officials failing to hear the emerging drumbeat of social change fail a key test of leadership. On the other hand the willingness of a public official to place his or her career on the line can become a wake-up call for both other legislators and the public to reconsider an issue.

On the other end of the scale lies the *delegate*, who sees his or her job as purely representing the communicated wishes of his or her constituents without second-guessing the wisdom or practicality of the course of action they suggest. The delegate figuratively raises his or her finger in the air to see which way the wind is blowing, exhibiting significant trust in the wisdom of the public. Delegates accept the dictum that democracy is the suspicion that more than half the interested and aware public is right more than half the time.

The Achilles heel of the delegate position lies in the fact that the public can be demonstrably wrong. In 2000, a swarm of e-mail messages generated communications to Congress asking members to block the five-cent proposed tax on e-mails. Legislation was drafted to stop the tax. The only problem was that the initial e-mails raising the issue were hoaxes as no tax had been proposed. In essence, due to constituent pressure, thousands of hours were spent to block government action that had never been proposed. Congressmen protected their constituents from a threat that did not exist.

The public sends mixed signals on what it expects. Polls show that 38% of adults feel their representative should "do what is best for the district" even if it is not good for the nation, while 52% feel representatives "should do what is best for the country as a whole even if it does not help the district" (University of Maryland).

The Inevitable Compromises

There are few absolute trustees or absolute delegates in legislative bodies. Many legislators shift their standard operating procedures based on the nature of the issue being considered. Domestic issues are much more likely to engage the interests of constituents and generate pressure for delegate-like behavior, while foreign policy issues often allow legislators more leeway to act as trustees. More junior and/or electorally insecure members stick closer to their constituent's views, while more senior and/or politically secure members fear constituents less and gravitate toward the trustee position (Kingdon, 242–261).

The New Media Environment: Cracking the Cooling Saucer

There is a legend that on his return from France, Thomas Jefferson called George Washington to account for having agreed to a second legislative chamber. "Why" asked Washington "did you pour your coffee into your saucer?" "To cool it," said Jefferson. "Even so," said Washington, "we pour legislation into the senatorial saucer to cool it." (Conway, 91) The quote has been used regularly to justify those aspects of the Senate (long terms of office, closed session, etc.) that keep the public at arm's length. The Senate and less often, the House, still carry out some business behind closed doors (such as national security issues). But the tide of transparency to the public has been sweeping in the opposite direction.

Secret police, punishment without public charges and trial, and secret deals lack legitimacy in the American mind. Our conception of sovereignty of the people demands a respect for their intelligence and capability to make important judgments. Woodrow Wilson transplanted this concept of openness into the international realm. The first of his Fourteen Points promised "Open covenants of peace, openly arrived at" (Wilson).

In an incongruous endorsement from a denizen of one of our most secret political institutions, Supreme Court Justice Louis Brandeis argued, "Publicity is justly commended as a remedy for social and industrial diseases. Sunlight is said to be the best of disinfectants; electric light the most efficient policeman" (Brandeis, p. 92).

In one sense Congress, and generally state legislatures, have been some of the most open of our political institutions, with their public galleries and detailed written records of activity. Until relatively recently, though, the access to public galleries or written records was limited to those who could travel to Washington or get to one of the federal depository libraries that received records months after an event. Two intertwined applications of technology increased the potential for well-informed constituents armed with current information. Real-time televising House (1979) and Senate (1986) sessions and committee meetings provided access to the political process while it was taking place. Constituents could follow debates and communicate with their legislators before a decision had been made. About the same time, Congress began to provide access to its records via the Internet. Cleverly named for Thomas Jefferson, who donated his personal library to populate the Library of Congress shelves and who allegedly asserted that "Information is the currency of democracy" (www.monticello.org/library/reference/spurious. html), the "Thomas system" (www.thomas.loc.gov) provides access to bill drafts, the *Congressional Record,* member biographies, the status of legislation, and dozens of other pieces of information useful for keeping an eye on Congress. As one Member summed up the changes he pointed out, "less is done by stealth today."

While no one publicly argues for a return to days of more secrecy, compromises are more difficult to make in the glare of public sunshine. One of Congress's reactions to the competing demands to "get something done," but "don't do that," is the new form of sleight of hand, omnibus legislation (see Box). By throwing together legislation on a large number of issues into one bill, it is hoped that the positive will outweigh the negative in the minds of a majority of members. Innocuous or misleading bill titles provide "cover" for members committed to getting something done. It was pretty hard to vote against the PATRIOT Act without having to justify one's patriotism. Yet for many, the act undermined civil liberties and included unpatriotic aspects. The Bipartisan Campaign Reform Act included the loaded words of "reform" and "bipartisan," but in reality only involved minimal voting across party lines and was seen by some as causing more problems than solutions.

Driving the Omnibus

Everyone likes a "win-win" situation. Omnibus legislation is the closest that legislative bodies get to that goal. In Latin, "omnibus" means "for all, for everyone." Omnibus bills combine together a wide range of mandatory or highly desirable legislation with more questionable offerings that may well be voted down if they faced a decision in isolation. Omnibus legislation is particularly important under conditions of divided government and/or slim partisan majorities. Omnibus appropriations bills at the end of the fiscal year often become important vehicles for all types of legislation since, without passage, the government would shut down. For example, the 2008 Omnibus Appropriations Bill was over 3,500 pages long and weighed over 25 pounds. Clearly no member could have read and digested it all. It included the $70 billion President Bush wanted for the war in Iraq and funding for fourteen government departments. The majority Democrats, on the other hand, inserted $11 billion in emergency spending for veterans, money for drought relief, heating subsidies, local law enforcement, Amtrak, programs for the poor, and housing. On the individual level, the omnibus bill included $7.4 billion to cover 8,983 largely hidden "earmarks"—local public works projects targeted for specific congressional districts—especially those represented by members from the majority party and serving on key committees.*

While strategically advantageous, omnibus legislation often means that significant portions of the budget are not carefully considered by all members. The temptation and reality push members toward looking for just enough good to outweigh the less desirable part of the legislation.

*Associated Press, "Senate Approves $70 Billion War Funding for Iraq, Afghanistan," available at www.foxnews.com

Helping the Process Along

The individual citizen often lacks the time, skill, or knowledge to hold public officials responsible (see Arnold, 1990 on inattentive publics). Interest groups allow individuals to pool their knowledge and resources to monitor, inform, and move government officials in new directions. We are all associated with "special interests" through our jobs, hobbies, clubs and/or religious organizations. Some of these interest groups are small and unorganized, while others have large professional staffs and massive budgets. Watching over the shoulders of elected officials, they have the ability to uncover decisions that support or undermine the interests they are bound to promote. The interest group process does not always work ideally. Some interest group leaders themselves fail to faithfully represent the interest of their members. The interest group playing field is not even. Groups with significant economic interests that are made up of well-off participants often have more resources than other groups. Some interests lack any organization. Elected officials tend to respond to those groups making the most noise, assuming that the lack of organization and activity implies lack of interest.

If all interest groups were equally organized and politically capable, their contribution to the "marketplace of ideas" would raise few questions. In reality, level of organization and group resources have little to do with the importance of the policies they prefer or the needs of the country. Some of the interests most in need of government help (consumers, the poor, children, etc.) pale in comparison to groups representing the wealthy, professionals, and the single-minded.

The Ethics of Constituency

While we normally think of ethics as applying to individuals holding official government positions, constituents also have ethical requirements when they enter the public sphere. It is natural to see ethics as a one-way street, applying to them, but not to us. Democracy, however, is a partnership with citizens having ethical constraints also.

Representing Reality   Government or private organizations (interest groups, corporations, political parties, etc.) cannot be everywhere all the time. Constituents are the eyes and ears of government touting successes and pointing out failures. In a democracy, constituents expend most of their effort reporting *on* government transgressions compared to repressive societies where some citizens relish reporting *to* government about the purported transgressions of their fellow citizens. The monitoring role of constituents serves as a quality-control check on government performance.

Unselfish Selfishness   While dictums such as "do the right thing," and "love your neighbor" waft through the body politic, many people see too many examples of selfishness to trust in the universality of these principles. It often takes an outsider to recognize that which is right before our eyes. French social observer Alexis de Toqueville in his 1831 voyage of discovery through a young United States gave an answer to the conundrum of how self-interest might result in unselfish acts when he talked about "self interest rightly understood." In his words:

> The Americans, on the contrary, are fond of explaining almost all the actions of their lives by the principle of interest rightly understood; they show with complacency how an enlightened regard for themselves constantly prompts them to assist each other, and inclines them willingly to sacrifice a portion of their time and property to the welfare of the state. (Tocqueville, 647)

In practical application, a constituent might accept his legislator's support for increased spending on low-income schools, even if he or she has no children to be educated. It is in the constituent's interest to educate the next generation, or at a minimum to keep "those" kids off the street. I may like my big SUV but support a tax break for hybrid cars recognizing the potential for gas-savings hybrids to reduce fuel demand, gasoline prices, and air pollution.

Making the Best Case   When entering a policy debate, a constituent has a variety of weapons to employ. Information is a crucial resource shepherded and carefully parceled out as the debate progresses. While the policy discussion would improve if all the players shared all the information, few want to give up a political advantage. A key ethical decision involves how much information one is willing to share. "Laying one's cards on the table" can be a strategic disadvantage. Another way to prove a point is to threaten political repercussions. Withholding votes, contributions, or other forms of support in order to get one's way may be effective, but may be used to promote unwise policies. Political participants must dig deep into their own souls to determine whether their policy goals are important enough to diminish the policy-making process or to have decisions based less on their merits than on present political conditions.

Playing Nice   Caught in the fever pitch of political preferences, it is possible to fall victim to a perspective that the ends justify the means. Approaching a legislator with threats, protests, or violent demonstrations may in some cases be legitimate, but it is important to remember that any strategy you wish to employ must also be granted your worst political enemy. Advocates of one position have no more right to testify at a hearing, give a campaign contribution, or disrupt committee meeting than do advocates of the opposite position. Democracy works best when advocates present competing positions on issues over which reasonable people disagree, and carry out their disagreement in an agreeable manner.

Cases of Re-presentational Conflict

Few issues challenge the representational role of members of Congress as deeply as war and peace. Historically, Congress has only formally declared war five times (the War of 1812, the Mexican-American War, the Spanish-American War, World War I, and World War II), although presidents have sent U.S. troops into harm's way over two hundred times. Although Congress's specific constitutional power to "declare war" has become largely unworkable in the modern world with the need for speed and secrecy, numerous equivalents to the declaration of war continue. War votes tend to be clear and public leaving little "wiggle room." They do not represent all the situations of representation, but do bring some of the most challenging into stark focus.

Woman in the Hall   Arriving in Congress in 1917, Jeannette Rankin (R-MT) became the women's caucus's only member. Montana's independent spirit and early decision to allow women to vote allowed this activist teacher and social worker to become the first female member of Congress. Growing up in a pioneer state where men and women worked shoulder to shoulder, Rankin was brought up to accept equality as the norm. She had facilitated her election by becoming an active spokesperson for women's right to vote. Her first vote defined her when she joined fifty-five male members in opposing U.S. entry into World War I. Both the public in general and her Montana constituents had second thoughts concluding, "women were incapable of shouldering the difficult burdens of national leadership" (www.history.com). Her Montana constituents rejected her bid for a seat in the Senate in 1918, based largely on her pacifist vote. In a case of history repeating itself, Rankin won a seat in the House again in 1940 as World War II was heating up. With the bombing of Pearl Harbor, pacifism seemed unreasonable to most of her constituents, but Jeannette Rankin marched forward with the sole dissenting vote on U.S. entry into the war in 1941. She thus became the only person to vote against both wars. Her constituents were less than pleased. Seeing the political handwriting on the wall, she decided not to run for re-election in 1942. In one sense she has maintained her position in the Capitol, this time as one of the two statues Montana is allotted.

Splitting the Difference   Senator William Fulbright (D-AR) wore the banner of being a Rhodes Scholar and intellectual with pride. He fully believed that "individual interests . . . were inextricably bound up with the well being of the community" (Fulbright quoted in www.encyclopediaofarkansas.net). Perhaps recognizing competing views of the public interest, Fulbright took seemingly competing positions on the two key issues of his time: the conflict in Vietnam and civil rights. While most of his Arkansas constituents showed consistency with the conservative perspective by supporting U.S. involvement in Vietnam and by opposing the civil rights movement, Fulbright picked and chose the views he would follow.

When it came to civil rights, Fulbright, personally a moderate, voted the pro-segregationist conservative position until the 1970s, more as a matter of political survival than conviction. In 1956, he signed the Southern Manifesto committing himself to use every legal tactic available to countermand the 1954 Supreme Court decision in *Brown v. Board of Education* promoting school desegregation. The political wisdom of this stand was borne out in 1958 when Louisiana Congressman Brooks Hays, a notable holdout in signing the Southern Manifesto, went down to defeat in an almost unprecedented, last-minute, write-in campaign.

One might expect Fulbright, a courtly southern politician, to unflinchingly stand for flag and country when it came to the policy toward Vietnam. As Chairman of the Senate Committee on Foreign Relations, he was in a premier position to challenge presidential initiatives in foreign policy, and he pulled few punches. Fulbright was the first senator to clearly break with U.S. policy in Vietnam, overseeing nationally televised investigations and proposing legislation calling presidents to account. Fulbright bristled over the fact that he and Congress had been misled by the Johnson administration and believed that the U.S. felt no threat and had no role to play in Vietnam.

Castigated for his stands, Fulbright argued that "In a democracy, dissent is an act of faith. Like medicine, the test of its value is not in its taste, but its effects" (http://www.answers.com/topic/j-william-fulbright). An effective politician, Fulbright recognized he had considerable leeway to act as a trustee on foreign policy issues, while toeing his constituents' line as a delegate on civil rights.

His political instincts prevailed in 1968 when he received 59% of the vote in his reelection bid, but the growing consternation of his constituents failed to evaporate. The lingering feeling among his constituents that he abandoned them resulted in them sending him packing after the 1974 election. His growing divergence from his constituents on issues such as Vietnam, led to his defeat by Dale Bumpers in the 1974 Democratic primary.

A New Lincoln   Abraham Lincoln asserted, "A house divided against itself cannot stand." His namesake, Senator Lincoln Chaffee (R-RI), took a new twist to determine whether a senator divided against his party and constituents can remain standing. A politician's political base begins with his or her party. It did not take long for Chafee to gain the moniker "RINO" (Republican In Name Only). As the most liberal Republican in the Senate, Chafee offended his fellow partisans yet was not fully trusted by the Democrats.[3] While Republicans in Rhode Island are relatively liberal, they are still Republicans with loyalty to the party.

Following his father into office, first by appointment and then by election, Chafee never had to build a strong constituent coalition. He arrived in the Senate feeling that the Bush administration "tore our best campaign promises to shreds and the moderate acquiesced instead of pelting him with outrage" (Press).

It was no surprise that Chafee would be the only Republican voting against the 2002 authorization to use force in Iraq. Chafee argued that he had made two "tortuous votes [but] this wasn't one of them" (http://freerepublic.com/focus/f-news/11797442/posts). The bipartisan support for the resolution was strong enough that the Republican leadership simply wrote him off. In the 2004 election, Chafee refused to vote for George W. Bush, casting a write-in ballot for Bush's father instead.

In 2006, Chafee successfully beat back a tough primary opponent by receiving strong support from Independents. He faced a Democrat in the general election who would largely be his clone in Senate voting. Since Chafee himself was much more popular than the Republican Party, a major issue was the possibility that defeating Chafee could lose the Republicans their majority in the Senate. A combination of disaffected Republicans, Independents, and loyal Democrats proceeded to hand Chafee a defeat after one term in office. One could say Chafee took being a trustee to the extreme.

No Vice   In 2000, Senator Joe Lieberman stood out as one of the two favored sons in the Democratic Party as their vice-presidential standard bearer. When that year's presidential election came down to the wire, with the result hinging on a recount in Florida, the taste of victory encouraged drastic tactics. Both parties attempted to interpret the rules in favorable ways. Florida became a "spin zone" where hundreds of spokespersons tried to interpret arcane laws, employ traditional ways of handling ballots, and demand the arguments of their opponents.

Supporters of the Gore-Lieberman ticket honed in on absentee ballots, many of which were from the military and presumably Republican. With the outcome of the election hanging on a few votes in Florida, members of the Gore-Lieberman team were unwilling to lose the election in that last moment by not taking advantage of every strategic advantage. Rejecting as many military ballots as possible seemed like a small price to pay for protecting the nation from George W. Bush. Given the large number of military bases and the Florida tax laws which forgive income tax for members of the military, the potential for a large number of military ballots is large. Military ballots were particularly susceptible to rejection since the laws failed to take into account the difficulty of submitting ballots from overseas. Difficulty in getting ballots postmarked, filled out completely, and delivered before the deadline loomed large. Party-appointed election judges allowed their partisan preferences to color their decision process. In heavily Democratic Dade County, local officials rejected 80% of the overseas ballots. In heavily Republican Jackson County, the rejection rate stood at 20%. Unless one concludes that overseas voters are selectively incompetent by county, something else was going on. Both sides had the motivation and the means to legitimately question such ballots. Lieberman became the point man and voice of reason, discouraging disenfranchisement of those who were defending our country on the basis of minor technicalities. The counting procedures were revised to provide more leniency for military ballots. Bush eventually won the electoral votes of Florida by a few hundred votes and went on to become president, while Gore was left with little more than bragging rights for having won a majority votes nationwide. It was not the first nor the last time Lieberman would take a principled stand offending many of those around him.

When the Senate voted to authorize the use of force in Iraq, Lieberman joined 29 other Democrats in their support. Over the next few years, virtually all of the other Democratic supporters of the Bush policy attempted to evade responsibility for their vote, while Lieberman continued his strong support for U.S. military involvement in the Middle East.

Senator Lieberman's position was particularly remarkable given the liberal and independent voting traditions of Connecticut. In previous years it had elected an Independent governor and was the home of Lowell Weicker, a liberal Republican Senator. Despite his strong record on other liberal causes, constituents were quick to point out that "Joe isn't listening to us"(AP). Given the votes associated with the war, Lieberman was ranked as the ninth most conservative Democratic member of the Senate in 2006, placing him closer to southern and Midwestern conservatives rather than to the more typical northeastern liberal wing of the party.[4]

Lieberman's initial challenge came at the Democratic state convention, which was seen as a referendum on the war in Iraq. The convention refused to give him the party nomination. Entering the party primary, Lieberman was again unable to overcome the disgust with his vote among party activists. Losing the party nomination and the primary to a newcomer (Ned Lamont), the chastised but unbowed Senator ran as an independent in the general election. With an almost non-existent Republican challenger and support from independents, Lieberman was able to win when it counted. For the time being he was able to maintain his independence. Returning to the Senate, he faced a number of colleagues who had actively campaigned for his Democratic challenger. In the 2008 presidential election, Lieberman endorsed his compatriot on the war, John McCain, and was even given a prime time spot during the Republican National Convention. The Democratic Leadership in the Senate loudly took note of his disloyalty. Eschewing a switch to the Republican Party, Lieberman remained a trustee seeking to educate and guide his constituents.

A Re-presentational Reprise

Representative democracy is not a spectator sport. It requires the involvement of all the players. Citizens who fail to get involved not only forfeit their right to complain, but more importantly fail to inform the policy dialogue and diminish their chances to have their policy preferences prevail. Legislators have the duty to reach out to constituents either to adopt their views (the delegate approach) or to educate their constituents on their own preferences (the trustee position). We all have a stake in a policy process that is transparent, based on valid information, and contested in a reasonable way that leads to enlightenment and acceptable compromise.

Notes

1. The guidance comes from the ethics of accepting a date to the dance. It is considered poor form to dump your date and go off with someone else.
2. Complete speech available at: http://press-pubs.uchicago.edu/founders/documents/v1ch13s7.html
3. See the *National Journal* scores at http://www.pollster.com/blogs/national_journal_2006_liberalc.php
4. See the *National Journal* scores at http://www.pollster.com/blogs/national_journal_2006_liberalc.php

References

Arnold, R. Douglas, *The Logic of Congressional Action*, New Haven, Yale University Press, 1990.

Associated Press, "Sen. Lieberman Beats Challenger Lamont in Connecticut," November 7, 2008.

Brandeis, Louis D. *Other People's Money and How the Bankers Use It*, New York: Frederick A. Stokes Co. 1914.

Conway, Moncure D., *Omitted Chapters of History in the Life and Papers of Edmund Randolph*, 1888.

Kingdon, John, *Congressmen's Voting Decisions*, Anne Arbor: University of Michigan Press, 1989.

Mayhew, David, *Congress the Electoral Connection*, New Haven: Yale University Press, 1974.

McHenry, James, "Notes on the Constitutional Convention" first published in *The American Historical Review*, vol. 11, 1906, p. 618, included in *The Records of the Federal Convention of 1787*, ed. Max Farrand, vol. 3, appendix A, p. 85 (1911, reprinted 1934).

Pitkin, Hannah, *The Concept of Representation*, Berkeley: University of California Press, 1967.

Press, Eval. "Chafee Chastened," *The Nation*, February 14, 2008.

Tocqueville, Alexis de, *Democracy in America*. (Originally published 1835). Chicago: University of Chicago Press, 2000.

University of Maryland, national survey of 1,204 adults, 1999, available at http://www.policyattitudes.org.

Wilson, Woodrow, Joint Session of Congress, January 18, 1918.

www.history.com, "This Day in History," November 7, 1916.

Questions

1. Were the founders too optimistic or too pessimistic about the motivations of political activists?

2. Which method of represenatation (delegate or trustee) seems most ethical to you?

3. What should an elected official do if he or she totally disagrees with his or her constituency on a significant issue?

4. Outline a set of ethical guidelines for political protestors. When is protest legitimate? What forms of protest are ethical?

5. Omnibus legislation and its typical earmark components raise a number of issues:

> Is it ethical to trade a small, narrow benefit to one's constituency for legislation with wasteful programs or misguided sections?

> Is it ethical for earmarks to be distributed based on partisanship and power rather than objective need?

> Is it ethical to make public policy in a process that is not transparent to the public?

> Is good (ethical?) public policy uniformly good, or simply a tradeoff between the good and the bad?

PART THREE

EXECUTIVE BRANCH

Popular Democracy, Elite Influence, and Political Legitimacy—The Presidential Elections of 1824 and 1828

BRENDAN J. DOHERTY

The presidential elections of 1824 and 1828 were defining events in American political history. At the heart of these contests were the very questions with which the framers of the Constitution grappled in the summer of 1787 as they gathered in Philadelphia to debate popular democracy and the power of elites, Congress' influence on the executive, and the nature and workings of the Electoral College. These issues still resonate today, as they go to the heart of questions about the legitimacy and effectiveness of our presidential election process and the democratic nature of our system of government.

These two elections together marked the demise of King Caucus, the system through which members of Congress selected party nominees for the presidency, and, in effect, chose the president himself as well. The fracturing of the Democratic-Republicans, the dominant party of the day, resulted, and the Democratic Party was born in its wake, setting the stage for the two-party competition that has defined much of American political development. The controversial outcome of the election of 1824 illustrates the little-understood mechanics of the Constitution's provisions that guide the selection of a president and brings to the fore the question of just who should have the power of choosing our nation's leaders.

In the aftermath of the election of 1824, a brutally personal and negative campaign for the 1828 election began immediately, illustrating that recent complaints about the duration and incivility of political campaigns have direct antecedents in political practices during the early days of the republic. Progress toward greater popular say in the choices made by the Electoral College followed as well, as states throughout the union made sometimes unsteady progress toward the ideals of popular democracy. The result was the nation's first Western president who claimed to be the true representative of all the American people and strived to take political power from the hands of the nation's elite and give it to the public.

The compelling story of the presidential elections of 1824 and 1828 is not just a drama of the past. The tensions revealed here echo those brought into sharp relief by the presidential election of 2000, when for the fourth time in American history the Electoral College led to the selection of a president who had received fewer popular votes than his opponent. The framers' concerns that the president should not be too dependent upon the Congress have new saliency in light of the shifting balance of power away from Congress and toward the president in 21st century American politics. And the debates in the 1820s about the power of elites who supposedly know best and the influence of the people's will are directly connected to questions about the role of superdelegates in the Democratic party's current nominating process. The electoral contests of 1824 and 1828 and the tensions they reveal tap into fundamental questions of popular will, political legitimacy, and the ongoing American struggle to form a more perfect union.

IN THE BITTER YEARS BETWEEN the presidential elections of 1824 and 1828, supporters of John Quincy Adams attacked Andrew Jackson as an untrustworthy man with an explosive temper and a dangerous record that made him unfit to serve as president. Their attacks became quite personal, as they went so far as to call

Jackson's mother a "common prostitute" and accuse his wife Rachel of being a bigamist, which allegedly made Jackson her "paramour lover." Jackson's allies responded by accusing Adams of living in, "kingly pomp and splendor" at the public expense, and
alleged that he had "denounced the Roman Catholics as bigots,
worshippers of images, and declared that they did not read their
bibles." They even claimed that Adams had served as a pimp for the
czar of Russia years earlier while serving as ambassador to that
country, asserting that he had offered up one of his chambermaids
to serve the sexual needs of Czar Alexander (Remini, *Adams* 118–
125; Brands 62–65).

These rancorous exchanges were the legacy of one of the
most extraordinary presidential elections in American political history, which culminated when members of the House of Representatives assembled inside the snow-covered Capitol in Washington, D.C., on Wednesday, February 9, 1825, to choose the next
president of the United States. Senators and their guests packed the
galleries of the House chamber to watch Speaker of the House
Henry Clay of Kentucky, who himself had aspired to the presidency but had fallen short, preside over the historic session that
would choose another man to be the nation's next chief executive.
The chamber was filled with excitement as the vote neared (Remini, *Jackson* 11–12; Remini, *Adams* 72).

The mechanics of the American Constitution had triggered
this extraordinary session of the House of Representatives. For
only the second time in the history of the republic, a presidential
election was thrown into the House of Representatives, which
would choose the nation's chief executive.[1] And for the first of
four times in the course of our nation's development, as would
happen again in 1876, 1888, and 2000, the presidential candidate
who won the greatest number of votes from the people would be
denied the presidency.

Members of the House of Representatives had been called to
choose the president of the United States because no candidate
had received a majority of Electoral College votes the previous fall

in the presidential election of 1824. With the vote divided among four candidates—all the same political party, the Democratic-Republicans—Andrew Jackson, the popular general and hero of the Battle of New Orleans in the War of 1812, had received a clear plurality of the popular and Electoral College vote, running far ahead of his closest rival, Secretary of State John Quincy Adams, but had fallen short of the majority of the Electoral College vote necessary to be elected president. Thus, according to the 12th Amendment to the U.S. Constitution, the decision fell to the members of the House of Representatives to select the next president from among the top three finishers in the Electoral College vote, with each state casting an equal vote regardless of population (Ellis 35–51).

This high-stakes contest was not only a watershed event in American political development in its own right, but, along with the events of the ensuing four years, also serves to illustrate the tensions in our constitutional system between popular democracy and elite control. For at issue in the presidential elections of 1824 and 1828 were the very questions with which the framers of the Constitution had grappled in the steamy summer of 1787 as they debated the power of elites and the role of the public, Congress' influence on the executive, and the nature and workings of the Electoral College. These issues still resonate today, as they go to the heart of questions about the legitimacy and effectiveness of our presidential election process and the democratic nature of our system of government.

The Rise and Fall of King Caucus

How did the presidential election of 1824 come to be decided by the House of Representatives? The answer lies in the system of choosing presidential nominees that had been used for the prior quarter century—a system that crumbled in the years leading up to the 1824 election. When the framers of the Constitution gathered in Philadelphia in 1787, they considered and rejected the option of having the president selected by members of the legislative branch, due in part to concerns that the president should be independent from the Congress. Instead, they created the Electoral College, a system under which electors would be chosen by state legislatures, and they prohibited members of Congress from serving as electors. Once political factions in the early republic coalesced into two political parties, the Federalists of John Adams and Alexander Hamilton and the Democratic-Republicans of Thomas Jefferson and James Madison, each party then had to decide how to select its presidential nominee (Nelson 81–82; CQ Press 157).

To do so, both parties relied on the Congressional Nominating Caucus, derisively called King Caucus by its critics, who assailed it for its lack of popular accountability. In every election from 1800 through 1820, the members of each political party's congressional delegation gathered in a party caucus to choose their nominee for the presidency. With the decline of the Federalist party—in 1820, the Democratic-Republican nominee, James Monroe, faced no major opposition in the general election, winning 231 out of the 232 Electoral College votes—Democratic-Republican members of Congress in effect selected the president (Nelson 81–82; CQ Press 19–25).

As the political ambitions of those who hoped to be chosen as president in 1824 became clear, King Caucus fell apart. Five Democratic-Republicans were seen as contenders for the party's nomination for the presidency—Senator Andrew Jackson of Tennessee, Secretary of State John Quincy Adams of Massachusetts, Secretary of the Treasury William Crawford of Georgia, Speaker of the House Henry Clay of Kentucky, and Secretary of War John Calhoun of South Carolina. As Crawford seemed to have the most support among the party's representatives in Congress, the other candidates were reluctant to rely again on King Caucus to select the party's nominee. Even after Crawford suffered a severe stroke in 1823 that left him with impaired speech, vision, and mobility, he was considered the certain nominee if the party again chose its standard bearer through its congressional caucus (CQ Press 24–25; Remini, *Jackson* 15).

Supporters of the other candidates condemned King Caucus on grounds both principled and pragmatic. The Tennessee General Assembly, which sought to advance the candidacy of its favorite son, Jackson, passed a resolution declaring:

1. A caucus nomination is against the spirit of the Constitution.

2. It is both inexpedient and impolitic.

3. Members of Congress may become the final electors [if no candidate receives of majority of the Electoral College votes, throwing the election into the House of Representatives] and therefore ought not to prejudge the case by pledging themselves previously to support particular candidates.

4. It violates the equality intended to be secured by the Constitution to the weaker states.

5. Caucus nominations may, in time (by interference of the states), acquire the force of precedents and become authoritative and, thereby, endanger the liberties of the American people (qtd. in Nelson 85).

The Tennessee General Assembly went on to instruct its state's senators "to use their exertions to prevent a nomination being made during the next session of Congress, by the members thereof in caucus, of persons to fill the offices of President and Vice-President of the United States" (qtd. in Nelson 85). Supporters of other candidates, seeing the odds tilted decisively in favor of Crawford, also urged a boycott. Only 66 of the Democratic-Republican members of Congress, about one-quarter of the caucus, met to choose a party nominee in February of 1824. About three-quarters of the 66 members of Congress at the caucus hailed from only four states—Crawford's native Georgia, New York, which was the home of Crawford supporter Martin Van Buren, North Carolina, and Virginia. Their selection of the ailing Crawford was both unsurprising and perhaps even counterproductive, as many critics saw the process as unfair, unrepresentative, illegitimate, and damaging to Crawford's candidacy (Ornstein 31–32; Remini, *Jackson* 18–19; CQ Press 24). Jackson wrote that the caucus was, "the last hope of the friends of Mr. Crawford. . . . It appears to me that such is the feelings of the nation that a recommendation by a congressional caucus would politically damn any name put forward by it" (qtd. in Brands 382).

Jackson, Clay, and Adams refused to yield to the will of the fractured congressional caucus. With no national party organization that could help resolve the dispute over the nominating process, each continued his candidacy, and each was nominated for president by legislatures or party conventions in states where they found their greatest support. Calhoun, surveying the crowded field, left the presidential race to run for the vice presidency, which he would win with ease, leaving a four-way contest for the presidency in the fall of 1824 (CQ Press 24–25; Ornstein 32).

The Candidates and the Campaign of 1824

The four candidates for the presidency, all hailing from the same party but with distinct, often geographically-based, areas of support, each had their own arguments to support their candidacy for the highest office in the land. No one questioned the credentials of John Quincy Adams, the current secretary of state and son of the nation's second president, John Adams. The younger Adams had a distinguished diplomatic career, serving as the United States' ambassador to Russia and helping to negotiate the Treaty of Ghent that ended the War of 1812, before aiding President James Monroe in articulating the Monroe Doctrine. He advocated a strong role for the federal government in shaping the affairs of the nation, a view in sync with that of Clay, but one that clashed with the governing philosophies of Crawford and Jackson (Remini, *Adams*).

Adams was not a naturally warm person, and did not take to the back-slapping and social give and take that so often characterizes political exchanges. He acknowledged as much himself, writing, "I am a man of reserved, cold, austere and forbidding manners. My political adversaries say, a gloomy misanthrope; and my personal enemies an unsocial savage. With a knowledge of the actual defects in my character, I have not the pliability to reform it" (qtd. in Remini, *Jackson* 16). He went on to lament, "I well know that I never was and never shall be what is commonly termed a popular man" (qtd. in Remini, *Adams* 64). His distinguished record of public service, along with his current enviable post—the past three presidents, Jefferson, Madison, and Monroe, had all previously served as secretary of state, making the position widely considered to be the best stepping stone to the presidency—outweighed his personal shortcomings and made him a formidable contender for the office he sought. An Adams victory would represent the continuation of the domination of national politics by the young country's Eastern elite, as the first five presidents—Washington, Adams, Jefferson, Madison, and Monroe—had all hailed from Virginia and Massachusetts.

While Adams was popular in his native New England, he could not match the breadth of support in Congress and throughout the government enjoyed by William Crawford of Georgia, the Secretary of the Treasury. Crawford was the favorite of a group of "Old Republicans," also known as the "Radicals," who wished to see a relatively weak federal government and advocated a restrictive interpretation of the powers granted to the president and the Congress by the Constitution. Some speculated that his backers continued to support Crawford even after his severely debilitating stroke in part because they would not have minded an infirm president leading a feeble central government (Remini, *Jackson* 14–15).

Speaker of the House Henry Clay was a nationalist like Adams, believing in a strong role for the central government. He hailed from Kentucky, then part of the frontier of American territory, and dreamed of being the nation's first Western president. His best hope for winning the presidency lay with the possibility of no candidate achieving an Electoral College majority, thereby throwing the election into the House, where he believed he could use his influence among his fellow members of Congress to engineer his own selection as president (Remini, *Jackson;* Remini, *Adams*).

Clay was not, however, the only candidate from the West. Andrew Jackson of Tennessee had captured the imagination of much of the public and was seen by many as an American hero. Born in a rural area in the Carolinas, he had moved to Tennessee as a young man, where he rose to lead the Tennessee militia first against Indians in the West, and then commanded the efforts to defend the Mississippi River from British aggression during the War of 1812. His victory in the Battle of New Orleans in January of 1815 thwarted British plans to control the Mississippi River from the Gulf of Mexico up through the heart of the North American continent to connect with their forces in Canada and cordon in the young and growing United States. While this battle is most often remembered in modern times for being fought after the Treaty of Ghent had been signed to end the war, as word of the treaty had not yet reached New Orleans, its significance is much greater. The battle stopped the British attempt to seize the Mississippi and fence in the ambitious yet fledgling American states, and gave the country a much-needed victory that provided a substantial boost to national morale after a long and difficult war (Brands).

Supporters hailed Jackson as a leader in the tradition of George Washington, and thought that his military heroism, bolstered by service in both the House of Representatives and the U.S. Senate, made him an ideal national leader. Critics saw him as an uneducated backwoodsman who rode a dangerous swell of popular passion to achieve political power—just the kind of popular demagogue that some of the framers of the Constitution had feared when they had considered and rejected the direct election of the president by the people (Brands).

Campaigns for the presidency in the early 1800s bore little resemblance to the contests of today. Decorum dictated that candidates did not "run" actively for office. Instead, candidates would "stand" for office, staying on the sidelines as their supporters promoted their candidacy in their stead. In 1824, Jackson surprised some of the political world when he declared that he would make known his stance, "upon any political or national question . . . about which the country feels an interest," a substantial departure from the customs of the day under which candidates would shy away from any appearance of seeking office (Troy 15).

Jackson's detractors claimed that he was a mere "military chieftain" whose temper and lack of experience made him a dangerous choice for president, while his supporters countered these attacks by portraying him as a heroic and noble figure who would be beholden to no special interest, and instead, would be the people's voice in Washington (Ellis). Jackson did not answer directly the criticisms made by his opponents, but he did from time to time suggest how his supporters might respond in his stead.

After Thomas Ritchie of Virginia accused Jackson of working with Adams and Calhoun against Crawford's candidacy, Jackson wrote to a friend, "Was I to notice the falsehoods and false insinuations of Ritchie and such unprincipled editors, I could have time for nothing else. Should you, upon reference to the piece alluded to, think it deserves any notice, such a one as the following might be proper: That General Jackson's course requires neither falsehood nor intrigue to support it. He has been brought before the nation by the people, without his knowledge, wishes, or consent. His support is the people" (qtd. in Brands 382). This claim of legitimacy based on the popular will would define Jackson's candidacy in 1824 and later his presidency.

The candidates' lack of public campaigning certainly did not mean that they did not take part in political intrigue. Adams, sensing a potential threat from Jackson and imagining a potentially unbeatable ticket if the New Englander could convince the Westerner to run with him as his vice presidential candidate, threw a ball for about a thousand guests in Jackson's honor in January of 1824, on the ninth anniversary of the triumph at the Battle of New Orleans. Jackson's polite toast to Adams at the ball appeared to indicate that he would be open to an alliance with Adams, but one never materialized, and the two candidates continued their rivalry for the presidency (Nagel 287–288; Remini, *Adams* 65).

The Election and the Electoral College

In the 1820s, elections for national office were not national elections at all, as voting for president did not take place on the same day across the country. Instead, on different days most states held elections in which voters cast ballots in support of electors pledged to vote for a certain candidate in the Electoral College (Nagel 291). The Constitution had left two important decisions to the states that bore directly on the question of electing a president—how to allocate Electoral College votes and which people would enjoy voting rights. Of the 24 states that then composed the federal union, 18 chose their electors in accordance with the popular vote. The six that did not—Delaware, Georgia, Louisiana, New York, South Carolina, and Vermont—instead placed the choice of electors in the hands of the state legislature. In the 18 states that selected electors in accordance with the will of the people, only certain people were permitted to participate at the ballot box. In the years leading up to the election of 1824, white males who did not own land had been allowed to vote in many, but not all, states alongside those who did hold property (Remini, *Jackson*).[2] While this move toward greater political participation was a step in the direction of fuller representation of the popular will, progress would be uneven and large segments of the population—most notably women and blacks—would still be excluded from the ballot box for decades to come.

By early December, the election results had come in, and as Table 1 illustrates, the popular vote tally favored Jackson, who received 151,271 votes. Adams finished second with 113,122 votes, almost 40,000 votes behind the general. Clay received the third most popular votes, with 47,531, while Crawford finished fourth, with 40,856 votes (CQ Press 112). There was a substantial lag between the time when the people or the legislature of each state voted and the announcement of the Electoral College vote. The Constitution stipulates that electors shall gather in each state to cast their votes, and that they shall then send the results of their balloting under seal to the president of the U.S. Senate, who is the vice president of the United States, an office held in 1824 by Daniel Tompkins.[3]

The sectionalism that divided the country on many political issues was apparent in December of 1824, when the Electoral College votes were finally received by Tompkins and counted. Jackson led the field with 99 out of the total of 261 Electoral College votes, with much of his support coming from the West and South. Adams, who drew most of his strength from the Northeast, finished second with 84 votes. Crawford, who came in fourth in the popular voting, managed a third-place finish with 41 Electoral College votes, most of which came from Virginia, New York, and

TABLE 1   The Presidential Election of 1824

Candidate	Popular Vote	Percentage	Electoral College Vote	Percentage
Andrew Jackson	151,271	41.3%	99	37.9%
John Quincy Adams	113,122	30.9%	84	32.2%
William Crawford	40,856	11.2%	41	15.7%
Henry Clay	47,531	13.0%	37	14.2%
Other	13,053	3.6%	0	0.0%
Total	365,833	100.0%	261	100.0%

Source: CQ Press, *Presidential Elections*, 112, 183.

his native Georgia. This left Henry Clay, the third place finisher in the popular vote, in fourth place in the tally that truly mattered with 37 Electoral College votes (CQ Press 183).

The switch in position of Clay and Crawford was of tremendous import, as the Constitution dictates that if no candidate wins a majority of the Electoral College vote, then the House of Representatives shall choose the president from the top three finishers. Clay, who finished third in the popular vote but fourth in the Electoral College count, was thus excluded from the coming balloting by the House, where many observers felt he might have been able to prevail had he been eligible.

Clay shared this opinion and lamented his near miss. His fate had been decided by Louisiana, one of the six states to allocate its electors by legislative decision instead of the popular vote. He wrote in a letter that, "Two of my friends in the Legislature were overset in a gig the day before and thereby prevented from attending; two others who were expected did not arrive. *Accident* alone prevented my return to the House of Representatives and, as is generally now believed, my election" (Brands 385–386). Had four members of the Louisiana legislature attended the pivotal session when electors were chosen, Henry Clay would have been one of the three candidates placed before the House of Representatives, and quite likely would have been chosen as the sixth president of the United States. Much to his chagrin, instead of remaining a candidate himself, Clay's influence would be critical in determining which of the other three candidates would become the next president of the United States.

The Origins of the Electoral College

How did the election of 1824 come to be decided by the elected members of the House of Representatives? The answer lies in the proceedings of the Constitutional Convention in the steamy summer of 1787. The fifty-five delegates who gathered in Philadelphia from May through September considered various methods of selecting the nation's chief executive, and only settled on the Electoral College during the closing days of the convention. What did the framers of the Constitution intend when they created the Electoral College?

It is tremendously difficult to evaluate the intent of the framers of the Constitution. The first question to confront is whose intent should matter: The fifty-five delegates to the Constitutional Convention? Or only the thirty-nine who signed the final document? Or the eight delegates to the convention who had previously signed the Declaration of Independence? Should one also take into account the will of the hundreds of citizens who participated in state conventions to ratify the new Constitution? What of the views of key leaders from the founding generation like John Adams and Thomas Jefferson, who were abroad during the crafting of the Constitution (Dahl)?

If one can settle on just whose intent should matter most, how does one go about evaluating just what the framers wanted? No official record was kept of the proceedings of the Constitutional Convention. James Madison's notes, published forty years after the convention, are the most complete account of the discussions that summer, but there is no way to verify their accuracy. Should only the framers' opinions at the time of the convention count, or should we take into account their views on the Constitution later in life? The views of Madison, for example, shifted dramatically in the decades following the convention, as he displayed even greater trust in majority rule toward the end of his life than he did in 1787 (Glennon 5–6; Dahl 31–37).

While it is difficult to discern the intent of the framers, we can learn a great deal from the actions they took and the words they supposedly uttered at the Convention. In doing so, it is helpful to keep in mind that the overriding priority of most delegates to the convention was to arrive at a workable deal for the new Constitution that would help to ensure the survival of the young nation. While each person brought his own preferences to the table, the outcomes manifested in the final Constitution would be the result of numerous compromises. And no issues at the convention were more contentious than those of the influence of the populous states versus that of the smaller states, and the pivotal question of slavery (Longley and Braun).

Throughout the summer, the delegates discussed at length and voted multiple times on various plans for choosing the nation's president. James Wilson of Pennsylvania later told his state's ratifying convention, "The convention, sir, were perplexed with no part of this plan, so much as with the mode of choosing the president of the United States" (qtd. in Dahl 74). The option that seems most intuitive to many today, direct popular election of the president by the people, had its supporters but was also seen as highly problematic by a number of delegates. Madison argued in favor, declaring:

> With all its imperfections, I like best an election by the people, or rather the qualified part of them, at large. There are two objections against this mode which have weight. The first arises from the disposition in the people to prefer a citizen of their own state, and the disadvantage this would throw on the smaller states. Great as this objection might be, it is not equal to such as lie against every other mode which has been proposed. The second difficulty arises from the disproportion of qualified voters in the Northern and Southern states, and the disadvantages which this mode would throw on the latter. (qtd. in Butzner 97)

Direct election of the president by the people brought into play the two most contentious issues of the convention. First, delegates from the smaller states feared their voices would not be heard in a system that gave so much weight to the more populous states. Second, direct popular election would seem to benefit the Northern states, as Southern states were unlikely to allow their sizable population of slaves to vote. These questions had cropped up earlier in the convention when the delegates debated the contours of the national legislature. The Connecticut Compromise had established a House, in which population would determine representation, and a Senate, in which each state would have an equal vote. Southerners found themselves in the contradictory position of arguing that slaves should have no rights but should be counted for the purposes of apportionment of seats in the House of Representatives to give Southern states greater political power. The three-fifths compromise established that each slave would count as three-fifths of a person for the apportionment of seats to the states in the House of Representatives.

Madison did not mention, however, another key reservation held by a number of delegates who did not place their trust in the principle of popular sovereignty. George Mason of Virginia thought it was, "as unnatural to refer the choice of a proper character for chief Magistrate to the people, as it would be to refer a trial of colours to a blind man. The extent of the country renders it impossible for the people to have the requisite capacity to judge of the respective pretensions of the candidates." Elbridge Gerry of Massachusetts warned that, "The popular mode of electing the chief magistrate would certainly be the worst of all. . . . The people are uninformed and will be misled by a few designing men" (qtd. in Butzner 89, 95). Mason and Gerry feared that the people would be most aware of and familiar with candidates from their own state or region, and would be susceptible to the influence of demagogues. Better, they argued, that the choice of a president be placed in the hands of those who knew better.

Selection of the president by Congress was the other plan most heavily considered and debated at the convention. Roger Sherman of Connecticut argued, "For the Executive to be independent of the legislature would be the very essence of tyranny. The sense of the nation will be better expressed by the Legislature than by the people at large. The latter will never be sufficiently informed of characters, and besides will never give a majority of votes to any one man." Mason concurred, contending, "Election by the national Legislature is liable to fewer objections than any other method" (qtd. in Butzner 94).

Gouverneur Morris of Pennsylvania, who favored direct election of the president, argued that selection by the Congress would leave the president beholden to the legislature, warning of the "danger of intrigue & faction if the appointmt. [sic] should be made by the Legislature," and declaring, "the indispensable necessity of making the Executive independent of the Legislature" (qtd. in Best 100). Gerry echoed the concern that there would be "constant intrigue kept up for the appointment" as presidential hopefuls would curry favor with the members of Congress, undermining the proposed separation of powers within the federal government (qtd. in Glennon 8).

At the end of August, having voted down proposals to entrust the selection of the president to the people and to the Congress, the delegates to the Constitutional Convention created a special committee to consider the various options for selecting the president. On September 4, 1787, the committee reported back to the delegates and recommended that "Each State shall appoint in such manner as its Legislature may direct, a number of electors equal to the whole number of Senators and members of the House of Representatives to which the State may be entitled in the Legislature." The proposal provided that in the event that no candidate earned a majority of the Electoral College votes, the Senate would choose the president. James Wilson objected strenuously, arguing that this provision made him "obliged to consider the whole [proposed Constitution] as having a dangerous tendency to aristocracy; as throwing a dangerous power into the hands of the Senate." The proposal was revised to give the House of Representatives the role of choosing a president in the event that no candidate won an Electoral College majority, with each state casting an equal vote regardless of population, and the plan was subsequently approved (Dahl 75–76).

The framers did not clearly foresee how the Electoral College would function in practice, in large part because they did not anticipate the formation of national political parties. While the Electoral College gave more influence to the more populous states, some delegates assumed that the Electoral College balloting would rarely result in a majority for any one candidate. Thus, they anticipated that the Electoral College would in effect serve as a nominating process, with elections often thrown into the House of Representatives, where the small states would exercise the same voting power as the large states (Longley and Braun 26–27). The consensus that General George Washington would be elected the nation's first president regardless of the method of selection adopted by the convention left many delegates assured that any potential problems would not be encountered immediately. Indeed, it would not be until Washington left the political scene that the young nation would witness the dynamics of the Electoral College in a competitive election in 1796.

The Electoral College was a pragmatic and unconventional compromise. While it was the first choice of few delegates, it became an acceptable alternative to many once the convention could not agree on either direct election of the president or selection by the Congress. By allocating voting power in the Electoral College according to the number of seats each state held in the House and Senate, the delegates avoided reopening difficult questions surrounding small and large states and the issue of slavery. Instead, they built the Electoral College on already agreed upon compromises. By placing the selection of electors in the hands of the state legislatures, the framers allowed for the possibility of popular influence if the states so chose, while at the same time created a mechanism that could filter and temper the public will.

Critics of the Electoral College decry it as an 18th-century anachronism that does not always represent well the will of the people, as a system in which only votes in electorally competitive states truly matter due to the winner-take-all allocation of electoral votes adopted by all but a handful of states in modern times, and as an unnecessary, overly complicated, and confusing intermediary step in a presidential election. But for all these legitimate complaints, the Electoral College has served as a stable and largely successful method of electing a president for over 200 years. Its defenders claim that in spite of its apparent flaws, the Electoral College is superior to any of the available alternatives.[4]

The House of Representatives Shall Choose . . .

While Jackson had won clear pluralities in both the electoral and popular vote in the presidential election of 1824, his fate lay in the hands of the House of Representatives. Nothing in the Constitution provided clear guidelines as to how decisions should be made in the House. The 12th Amendment to the U.S. Constitution reads:

> "The person having the greatest number of [Electoral College] votes for President, shall be the President, if such number be a majority of the whole number of Electors appointed; and if no person have such majority, then from the persons having the highest numbers not exceeding three on the list of those voted for as President, the House of Representatives shall choose immediately, by ballot, the President. But in choosing the President, the votes shall be taken by states, the representation from each state having one vote; a quorum for this purpose shall consist of a member or members from two-thirds of the states, and a majority of all the states shall be necessary to a choice."

Thus, each state would cast one vote regardless of population, which meant that tiny Delaware, with three Electoral College votes, would wield the same influence in the final selection of the president as New York, the most populous state, which had 36 Electoral College votes. The Constitution provided no guidance on how congressional delegations from each state were to decide how to cast their vote. Should the members of the delegation hold an internal vote, and then cast their state's vote for the candidate who earned the most support? Or should they cast their state's vote in favor of the candidate who won that state's popular vote in the fall election? Ought they to follow the wishes of their state legislature? Did they have an obligation to support the candidate who won the popular vote nationwide? With the Constitution silent on these important questions, controversy and political intrigue would swirl around the decisions of the members of the House of Representatives.

While a presidential election had been decided by the House of Representative only once before, in 1800, and no other election had been thrown into the House since, it was all but inevitable that the House would again be called upon to decide a presidential election. Indeed, with only small changes in the national popular vote, numerous narrowly-decided elections throughout our nation's history could have ended up in the House of Representatives, including the contests of 1836, 1856, 1860, 1892, 1948, 1960, and 1968 (CQ Press 165). In each of these years, the nation only narrowly avoided having the presidential election decided by the federal government's legislative branch.

The Corrupt Bargain

Rumors of intrigue, backroom deals, bribery, and corruption beset the capital city as the vote on February 9, 1825, approached. Much discussion focused on whom Speaker Clay would favor, and supporters of each candidate made their case to the legislator from Kentucky. An associate of Jackson wrote to Clay, "My dear Sir, all our dependence is on you; don't disappoint us; you know our partiality was for you next to the Hero; and how much we want a western President." An advocate of Crawford wrote, "The hopes of the Republican party are concentrated on you. For God's sake preserve it—If you had been returned instead of Mr. Crawford every man of us would have supported you to the last hour. We consider him & you as the only genuine Republican candidates." Not to be outdone, a supporter of Adams wrote, "Sir Mr. Adams has always had the greatest respect for you, & admiration for your talent— There is no station to which they are not equal—Most undoubtedly you were the second choice of New England. And I pray you to consider seriously whether the public good & *your own future interests* do not point most distinctly to the choice which you ought to make [emphasis added]" (Remini, *Adams* 69).

Much speculation would swirl around whether Clay discussed concretely his "own future interests" with the candidates or their supporters as he made up his mind. In response to a request by Clay, he and Adams met privately in Adams's home on the evening of Sunday, January 9, 1825. What transpired there remains unknown. Adams wrote in his journal that Clay declared, "The time has come for me to make a decision," and asked Adams "to satisfy him with regard to some principles of great public importance, but without any personal considerations for myself." Adams recorded no more of what the two men discussed, but he did note that at the end of their discussion, Clay told the secretary of state that he "had no hesitation that his preference would be for me" (Remini, *Adams* 70).

On January 10, the Kentucky state legislature passed measures declaring that it "was the wish of the people of Kentucky" that the state's congressional delegation should cast their vote for Jackson, the candidate of the West. But Clay's influence prevailed, when on January 24, the members of the House from Kentucky announced that they would support Adams. Critics reacted swiftly. South Carolina's Robert Hayne indignantly responded, "We are in commotion about the monstrous union between Clay & Adams" (Remini, *Adams* 70–71).

Speculation about whether a bargain had been struck abounded, and on January 28, an anonymous letter was published in the Philadelphia *Columbia Observer* accusing Clay of agreeing to swing the election in the House to Adams in exchange for appointment in the coming administration as secretary of state. In response, Clay declared, "I pronounce the member, whoever he may be, a base and infamous calumniator, a dastard and a liar; and if he ever dare unveil himself and avow his name, I will hold him responsible . . . to all the laws which govern and regulate the conduct of men of honor." While the author, who was revealed to be Congressman George Kremer of Pennsylvania, later withdrew his accusation, the suspicions remained that Clay and Adams had struck a deal (Remini, *Jackson* 21–22; Brands 388).

Clay's writings indicate that his support for Adams was as much a rejection of Jackson as it was an endorsement of the secretary of state. Clay wrote in one letter, "Mr. Adams, you know well, I never should have selected if at liberty to draw from the whole mass of citizens for our President. But there is no danger in his elevation now or in time to come. Not so of his competitor, of whom I cannot believe that killing 2,500 Englishmen at New Orleans qualifies for the various, difficult, and complicated duties of the Chief Magistrate." In another missive, Clay wrote, "As a friend of liberty, and to the permanence of our institutions, I cannot consent, in the early stage of their existence, by contributing to the election of a military chieftain, to give the strongest guaranty that this republic will march in the fatal road which has conducted every other republic to ruin" (Brands 387). Clay clearly found Jackson's military credentials far less compelling qualifications for the presidency than did many members of the public.

Adams was not the only candidate who faced allegations of secret deals. One rumor held that Jackson had personally met with Crawford and proposed to give him "any terms . . . as the price of his cooperation and support." Van Buren, who managed the efforts to win support for Crawford, supposedly sought to negotiate patronage positions at the State Department with Adams, only to be told that Adams would talk with him about this only after the House had elected a president (Remini, *Jackson* 22).

Wednesday, February 9, 1825, arrived with the outcome of the election still very much in doubt. Due to Crawford's poor health, the decision appeared to be between Adams and Jackson (Ellis 40), but Van Buren hoped to deadlock the New York delegation and deny Adams or Jackson a majority in the first rounds of balloting, with the aim of swinging support to the incapacitated Crawford as a compromise choice if neither other candidate could muster majority support (Remini, *Adams* 72).

With 24 states then comprising the Union, the votes of 13 were necessary to be chosen president. Four states—Delaware, Illinois, Mississippi, and Missouri—had only one seat in the House of Representatives, and thus the sole congressman from each state would decide that state's vote. The other 20 states would decide how to cast each state's single ballot according to the results of an internal vote among their congressmen. Many observers expected that, as Van Buren hoped, no candidate would carry a majority of the states in the first rounds of balloting. They were mistaken. The key to the outcome lay in New York's divided delegation (Remini, *Adams* 71–72).

General Stephen Van Rensselaer of New York had promised not to vote for Adams in the first round of balloting. Van Rensselaer was concerned that an Adams presidency would exclude former Federalists like himself from positions of power and influence. While the Federalist party no longer had national reach, remnants still existed in certain states, including Maryland and Massachusetts, and its members and sympathizers were concerned that they would not benefit from patronage appointments under the next administration. Before the House voted, Van Rensselaer was summoned to Speaker Clay's office, where both Clay and Congressman Daniel Webster of Massachusetts urged the New Yorker to reconsider and support Adams on the first ballot. When he left Clay's office, he was supposedly heard grumbling that, "the vote of New York . . . depended upon him," and "if he gave it to A. [Adams] he could be elected most probably on the first ballot" (Remini, *Adams* 71–72).

When Van Rensselaer's turn came to cast his vote, he closed his eyes and bowed his head to pray. Upon opening his eyes, he saw a ballot for Adams lying on the ground by his seat. Taking this as an indication of divine will, he took the ballot and placed it in the ballot box. According to Van Buren, Van Rensselaer's vote was decisive, swinging New York and thus the presidency itself to Adams. The tally within the New York delegation was 18 votes for Adams, 14 for Crawford, and two for Jackson, giving Adams a one-vote absolute majority, and making the story of Van Rensselaer's divine inspiration and decisive vote a famous American political tale (Nagel 294; Remini, *Adams* 72–73).

On the first ballot, Adams prevailed with the minimum necessary majority of thirteen states, followed by seven for Jackson and four for Crawford. Adams carried the six states of New England—Maine, New Hampshire, Vermont, his native Massachusetts, Rhode Island, and Connecticut. Thanks in large part to Clay's support, he also received the votes of Kentucky, Missouri, Ohio, and Louisiana. Maryland, Illinois, and New York cast their votes for Adams as well, providing him with the margin of victory he needed. Andrew Jackson, who had won the national popular vote with almost 40,000 votes more than Adams had received, a margin of 10.4%, and who had led in the Electoral College tally by 15 votes, was denied the presidency (Ellis 50–55).

Upon hearing the results, supporters of Adams applauded vigorously, while a partisan of Jackson declared that, "The cards were stacked." Adams, who had reported to work at the State Department that day as per his regular routine, learned the news when an official delegation arrived to announce the outcome of the House vote. "May the blessing of God rest upon the event of this day!" Adams replied upon hearing of his selection (Remini, *Adams* 73).

That night, President Monroe held a reception to honor the president-elect. Both Adams and Jackson attended, and were courteous to one another and shook hands. "How do you do, Mr. Adams? I hope you are well, sir," said Jackson to his triumphant rival. "Very well, sir. I hope General Jackson is well!" replied Adams. Adams recorded that Jackson was, "altogether placid and courteous." One of Jackson's supporters in attendance was less polite. Referring to the decisive influence of the Speaker of the House, he grumbled, "There is our '*Clay President*,' and he will be moulded [sic] at that man's will and pleasure as easily as clay in a potter's hands" (Remini, *Jackson* 25; Brands 295; Remini, *Adams* 73).

Several days later, Adams and Clay met, and the President-elect offered the post of secretary of state to the Speaker of the

House. Clay took a week to give his response. While he desired the position, he knew that accepting it would raise a political outcry, as it would appear that he had indeed struck a deal with Adams. After much consideration, Clay concluded that he could not turn down the chance to serve the new administration, and accepted the position as the highest ranking member of Adams' cabinet (Remini, *Adams* 73–74).

Jackson's political allies levied charges that a "corrupt bargain" had been struck between Adams and Clay, and that their deal had subjugated the will of the people to the judgment of a cabal of corrupt politicians. Jackson himself was furious. He resigned his office in the United States Senate and returned to his native Tennessee. "Clay voted for Adams and made him president and Adams made Clay secretary of state. Is this not proof as strong as holy writ of the understanding and corrupt coalition between them," he wrote. "So you see the Judas of the West has closed the contract and will receive the thirty pieces of silver. His end will be the same. Was there ever witnessed such a bare faced corruption in any country before?" (Remini, *Jackson* 25; Remini, *Adams* 74). While Clay may have had many legitimate reasons for supporting Adams, not least of which their shared view that the national government should play an active role in developing the nation's economy, and although no one can know with certainty whether the two men struck a deal, the alleged "corrupt bargain" would haunt both of them throughout Adams's presidency and beyond.

The Presidential Election of 1828

The contentious presidential election of 1824 left its mark on contemporary politics and on American political development. While modern campaigns for the presidency are often decried as being far too lengthy, with virtually no time between campaigns devoted to the practice of governing (Ornstein and Mann), the ongoing rivalry between Adams and Jackson demonstrates that these are not exclusively modern dynamics. Jackson's supporters felt that he had been robbed and that the will of the people had been denied. In early 1825, Jackson returned to Nashville, and his supporters launched an active effort to capture the presidency in 1828, nearly four years later. Indeed, before John Quincy Adams was even inaugurated in 1825, the *Nashville Gazette* asserted that Jackson would be a candidate for the presidency in 1828.

While Jackson himself no longer worked in the nation's capital, his allies there continued to advance the cause of his candidacy. Senator John Eaton, Jackson's fellow Tennessean, spearheaded the purchase of a Washington newspaper that they would use to tout the General and attack his enemies. Sam Houston, who had served in the Tennessee militia with Jackson, became a member of Congress and wrote him that, "I have not in my life seen a cause rising so fast as that of the people is, nor one sinking faster than the cause of a wicked and corrupt coalition! . . . You lose no friends but gain daily. It will be so until the great day of deliverance to our country arrives" (Brands 389–391). Jackson's second campaign for the presidency, which would span Adams' four years in office, had begun.

Following the uproar around the outcome of the presidential election, the unsteady spread of popular democracy continued. Of the six states that in 1824 allowed their state legislatures to choose the allocation of their Electoral College votes, four of them—Georgia, Louisiana, New York, and Vermont—decided to let the outcome of the popular vote in the upcoming 1828 presidential election determine the choice of electors. This left only Delaware and South Carolina still selecting electors by legislative fiat instead of in accordance with the will of the people. By the election of 1832, only South Carolina continued the practice of legislative selection, which it would employ until after the Civil War. Due in no small part to the controversial election of 1824, the people would increasingly determine the allocation of Electoral College votes (CQ Press 161).

Adams came to regard his term as president as the most unhappy four years of his life, and his presidency would never escape the shadow of the "corrupt bargain" that many claimed had placed him in the White House. Supporters of Jackson organized to oppose the president from the opening days of his administration. While Clay was confirmed as secretary of state by the Senate, the 27 votes in favor and 14 votes opposed represented a remarkable level of opposition to a cabinet appointment. Adams saw the votes against confirmation as an attempt to advance, "the banners of General Jackson." Clay later acknowledged that accepting Adams' offer was the worst political mistake of his life (Nagel 296–298).

Congressional opposition to Adams and Clay stiffened over time. While Adams and Clay both advocated a strong role for the federal government, the allies of former Treasury Secretary Crawford and Vice President Calhoun allied themselves with the Jacksonians to promote what they saw as a vision of limited national government consistent with the philosophy of Thomas Jefferson. One such supporter called for electing Jackson president as the best method of ending the "cursed union of 'puritan and blackleg.' . . . He [Jackson] is the only man that can break down this union . . . [leading to] the substantial reorganization of the old Republican party" (Remini, *Adams* 84).

This opposition continued to use the label of the Democratic-Republican party, which would later become simply the Democratic party, while the allies of Adams and Clay called themselves National Republicans. On issue after issue, from internal improvements to tariff legislation, Indian removal, and foreign affairs, Adams encountered substantial organized opposition from a hostile Congress intent on both blocking his initiatives and promoting the prospects of Andrew Jackson in the upcoming election of 1828 (Remini, *Adams* 75–116; Ellis 41).

Modern political commentators who lament the demise of a long-ago era of civility in politics need to look no further than the presidency of John Quincy Adams to see that such longings are often based more on myth than historical fact. In one of the more outlandish accusations, Jackson's supporters alleged that years earlier Adams, in effect, had served as a pimp for the czar of Russia while serving as ambassador to that country, claiming that he had offered one of his servants to fulfill the sexual desires of Czar Alexander (Remini, *Adams* 118–119).

Supporters of Adams responded by attacking Jackson's wife, Rachel, as a bigamist. Before meeting Jackson, the former Rachel Donelson Robards had been married to Lewis Robards, who deserted her. Controversy still swirls over whether she had already been divorced from Robards when she and Jackson married. Partisans of Adams insisted that she had not been, and labeled Jackson her "paramour lover." When Rachel suffered a fatal heart attack on December 22, 1828, Jackson attributed her death to the stress placed upon her by the public smearing of her good name. Adams's partisans attacked not only Jackson's wife, but his mother as well. One pro-Adams newspaper ran the following item: "General Jackson's mother was a COMMON PROSTITUTE, brought to this country by the British soldiers! She afterward married a MULATTO MAN, with whom she had several children, of which General JACKSON IS ONE!!! [emphasis in original]" Jackson's supporters denied the charges (Brands 62–65; Remini, *Adams* 119–120).

The Jacksonians responded with assaults on both Adams's policy positions and his personal integrity, charging him with living like royalty at the expense of the public. Congressmen sympathetic to the General were urged to, "Push the enquiries about the money. Bring John Q's account before the Congress again if you can get them there—the whole from the commencement of the govt [sic] to the present day." They found that Adams had been paid on average $12,000 per year by the government since he was sent to serve as ambassador to Russia in 1809. Disdainfully they declared, "We disapprove the kingly pomp and splendor that is displayed by the present incumbent," emphasizing in a not-so-subtle manner the distinction between the aristocratic Adams and Jackson, the man of the people (Remini, *Adams* 120).

Divisive falsehoods were targeted toward specific segments of the population as well. Administration allies were accused of referring to the Dutch, who lived in substantial numbers in New York,

New Jersey, and Delaware, as, "the Black Dutch, the Stupid Dutch, and the ignorant Dutch and other names equally decorous and civil." Irish-Americans in cities including Boston and New York were informed, "Mr. Adams . . . [and] the partisans of Messrs. Adams & Clay . . . [had] denounced the Roman Catholics as bigots, worshippers of images, and declared that they did not read their bibles." They were also reminded of the religious discrimination they or their ancestors had suffered at the hands of the British crown, declaring, "Johnny Q. the tory [aimed to] UNITE CHURCH AND STATE after the manner of the English monarch," while at the same time touting that Jackson was "the son of honest Irish parents." In the West, where anti-Catholic sentiment was common, Jackson's supporters switched their approach and said that Adams associated with Catholic clergy, and that he spoke in Latin, as was done in a Catholic mass. (Remini, *Adams* 120–121).

In an era long before mass media, the vehicles for these charges were, in Adams's words, "pamphlets, newspapers, handbills, stump-speeches, and dram-shop dialogues, throughout the Union, and, in the face of fifty refutations, the skunks of party slander have been for the last fortnight squirting around the House of Representatives, thence to issue and perfume the atmosphere of the Union." Adams's friends employed similar tactics, using newspapers, handbills, and the like to portray Jackson as untrustworthy, with an explosive temper and a dangerous record. They publicized Jackson's supposed heavy-handedness as a military commander, the duel in which Jackson had killed a man years earlier over a bet on a horse race, the barroom brawl in his youth with future Senator Thomas Hart Benton, his treatment of Indians, and even his supposed alliance with former Vice President Aaron Burr, who had killed Alexander Hamilton in a duel and had allegedly conspired to sever parts of the southwestern United States with the goal of forming a new and separate country (Remini, *Adams* 120–125).

The Jacksonians worked hard to rally popular support for their candidate, building committees, often called Hickory Clubs after Jackson's battlefield nickname of Old Hickory, across the country at the local, county, and state levels. These committees planned rallies, parades, barbecues, and other vibrant events to build enthusiasm for the Hero of New Orleans. Adams's supporters, on the other hand, were disdainful of these efforts and made little attempt to build similar popular support for their candidate. Peter Force, editor of a newspaper in Washington, D.C., that supported the president, wrote, "The multiplication of Jackson meetings, and the number of which they are composed are favorite themes with the Opposition papers. . . . If we go into one of these meetings, of whom do we find them composed? Do we see there the solid, substantial, moral, and reflecting yeomanry of the country? No. . . . They comprise a large portion of the dissolute, the noisy, the discontented, and the designing of society" (Brands; Ellis 41; Remini, *Adams* 121–122).

The battle lines for the election of 1828 were clearly drawn. Supporters of Jackson portrayed Adams as an out-of-touch, aristocratic, elitist, in stark contrast with Jackson, whom they contended was a true man of the people who would govern with the best interests of the general public at heart. Partisans of Adams, for their part, charged that Jackson's background, judgment, and temperament made him unfit to serve as president. While there were disagreements over policy positions, the campaign was notable for its nasty, negative, personal nature (Ellis 43–59).

After four years of bitter opposition, Adams and Jackson at last faced off again in the fall of 1828. As he had in 1824, Jackson won the most popular and Electoral College votes, but this time his victory was decisive. He carried 56.0% of the popular vote to Adams's 43.6%, and took 178 Electoral College votes to Adams's 83 (CQ Press 113, 184). Jackson's triumph over Adams in 1828 marked the first time a Westerner and a relative political outsider was selected as our nation's chief executive, breaking the hold of Virginia and Massachusetts on the executive mansion.

Jacksonians contended that the 1828 election should be considered "by the sound planters, farmers & mechanics of the country as a great contest between the aristocracy and democracy of

America" (qtd. in Remini, *Adams* 118), and the unruly inaugural celebration at the White House would cement Jackson's image as the first president truly of the people. The public reception at the White House following Jackson's swearing-in at the Capitol was described by Margaret Bayard Smith:

> "What a scene did we witness! The *Majesty of the People* had disappeared, and a rabble, a mob, of boys, negros, women, children, scrambling, fighting, romping. What a pity, what a pity! No arrangements had been made, no police officers placed on duty, and the whole house had been inundated by the rabble mob. . . . Cut glass and china to the amount of several thousand dollars had been broken in the struggle to get to the refreshments, punch and other articles had been carried out in tubs and buckets. . . . Ladies fainted, men were seen with bloody noses, and such a scene of confusion as is impossible to describe" (qtd. in Brands 412).

Tales of this raucous celebration would come to take on legendary proportions, with Jackson's detractors citing it as just one of many reasons he was not fit to hold the presidency, while his supporters cast the unruly affair as an indication of Jackson's connection with the common people of the country.

As president, Jackson embraced the populism so evident in his campaign and his inaugural celebration, and in doing so, redefined presidential popular leadership. Jackson asserted that the president was "the direct representative of the people" (qtd. in Troy 15). He saw his presidency as one more step toward that more perfect union promised in the preamble to the Constitution. His primary goal was to take government out of the hands of the elites who had dominated the nation's politics and make the system more responsive to ordinary citizens. Jackson publicly laid claim to the mantle of national leadership, declaring that he, in stark contrast with the Congress, was the only official elected by all the people and thus represented the national interest, instead of particularistic local and regional concerns. Subsequent presidents have followed his lead (Brands 553–557; Dahl 69).

Jackson would serve in the White House for eight years, defeating his rival Henry Clay handily for the presidency in 1832. The followers of Jackson would become the modern Democratic party, and their ascendancy would mark the return to the two-party politics that has characterized most of American political history. The Whig party, which would later give way to the Republican party, was formed in the 1830s in direct opposition to Jackson's policies. Adams joined the Whig party after he was elected to the House of Representatives, where we would serve from 1831 until his death in 1848, becoming the only president to serve in the House after leaving the White House (Brands; Remini, *Adams*).

Jackson is widely considered the more accomplished president of the two men, and his image adorns the twenty dollar bill. In a 1996 survey of 32 prominent historians, Jackson was ranked as our fifth greatest president and was labeled "Near Great." Adams, on the other hand, was evaluated as "Average," coming in behind 17 other presidents (Schlesinger 189). While Adams's presidency was marked by frustration and, in some respects, failure, his lengthy career as a diplomat, president, and a congressman who worked tirelessly for the abolition of slavery earned him an honored place in American history (Remini, *Adams*).

While Adams and Jackson, the sixth and seventh presidents of the United States, were bitter rivals, they will be forever linked in history. It was in 1824 that, for the first of four times in American history, the candidate who won the most votes did not end up in the White House. The controversial proceedings in the House of Representatives paved the way for the election of 1828 and several watershed changes in American political development. While the framers had debated the proper balance between popular will and elite control, following the election of 1824 the scales would be permanently tipped in favor of the people. Although undemocratic elements of our electoral processes endure, from the Electoral College to the use of superdelegates in the Democratic party's nominating process for the presidency, the elections of 1824 and 1828 would bring to the fore the issue of legitimacy in a democratic republic.

Notes

1. In 1800, Thomas Jefferson and Aaron Burr, both Democratic-Republicans running on the same ticket, had tied in the Electoral College with each receiving 73 votes. Since the Constitution originally provided that the first place finisher in the Electoral College would be elected president with the runner-up becoming vice president, the election was sent to the House of Representatives, where Jefferson was elected on the 36th ballot, with Burr becoming the vice president. This election would lead to the adoption of the 12th Amendment to the Constitution which called for the separate election of president and vice president (CQ Press 19–20).
2. For more on the struggle over the expansion of suffrage, see the discussion of Rhode Island's Dorr Rebellion in part one of this volume.
3. This constitutional arrangement would lead to an awkward scene 176 years later, when then-Vice President Al Gore received the disputed Electoral College votes in the 2000 election that resulted in George W. Bush's selection as president.
4. For discussion of the merits and defects of the Electoral College, see Polsby, Wildavsky, and Hopkins (2007) and chapters within Ellis and Nelson (2006).

References

Best, Judith A. *The Choice of the People? Debating the Electoral College.* Lanham, MD: Rowman & Littlefield Publishers, Inc., 1996.

Brands, H. W. *Andrew Jackson: His Life and Times.* New York: Doubleday, 2005.

Butzner, Jane. *Constitutional Chaff: Rejected Suggestions of the Constitutional Convention of 1787 With Explanatory Argument.* New York: Columbia University Press, 1941.

CQ Press. *Presidential Elections, 1789–2000.* Washington, DC: CQ Press, 2002.

Dahl, Robert A. *How Democratic is the American Constitution?* 2nd ed. New Haven: Yale University Press, 2003.

Ellis, Richard E. *Andrew Jackson.* Washington, DC: CQ Press, 2003.

Ellis, Richard J. and Michael Nelson, eds. *Debating the Presidency: Conflicting Perspectives on the American Executive.* Washington, DC: CQ Press, 2006.

Glennon, Michael J. *When No Majority Rules: The Electoral College and Presidential Succession.* Washington, DC: Congressional Quarterly, Inc., 1992.

Longley, Lawrence D. and Alan G. Braun, *The Politics of Electoral College Reform.* New Haven, CT: Yale University Press, 1975.

Nagel, Paul C. *John Quincy Adams: A Public Life, A Private Life.* New York: Alfred A. Knopf, 1997.

Nelson, Michael, ed. *The Evolving Presidency: Landmark Documents, 1789–2008.* 3rd ed. Washington, DC: CQ Press, 2008.

Ornstein, Norman. "Three Disputed Elections: 1800, 1824, 1876." *After the People Vote: A Guide to the Electoral College.* Ed. John C. Fortier. Washington, DC: The AEI Press, 2004.

Ornstein, Norman, and Thomas Mann, eds. *The Permanent Campaign and Its Future.* Washington, DC: American Enterprise Institute and the Brookings Institution, 2000.

Polsby, Nelson W., and Aaron Wildavsky, with David A. Hopkins. *Presidential Elections: Strategies and Structures of American Politics.* 12th ed. Lanham, MD: Rowman and Littlefield Publishers, 2007.

Remini, Robert V. *The Election of Andrew Jackson.* Philadelphia, PA: J.B. Lippincott Company, 1963.

Remini, Robert V. *John Quincy Adams.* New York: Times Books, Henry Holt and Company, 2002.

Schlesinger, Arthur M., Jr. "Rating the Presidents: Washington to Clinton." *Political Science Quarterly* 112.2 (1997): 179–190.

Troy, Gil. *See How They Ran: The Changing Role of the Presidential Candidate.* Cambridge, MA: Harvard University Press, 1996.

Questions

1.   Was there anything unethical or illegitimate about Adams's selection as president? Were any rules broken? Does your answer change if you assume that Clay was or was not promised the office of secretary of state in exchange for his support of Adams in the House? Are the rules governing the selection of a president if no candidate earns an Electoral College majority themselves legitimate?

2.   The framers of the Constitution wrestled with the tensions between popular sovereignty and elite control. Did they strike the proper balance? Would our system function better if the president were elected by the Congress today? Or directly by the people?

3.   The Electoral College process has resulted in a president who didn't win the popular vote four times in the 56 presidential elections held between 1789 and 2008. What are the negative elements of this system of choosing a president? What arguments can be made in its defense?

4.   If no candidate for president earns an Electoral College majority and the selection of the nation's chief executive falls to the House of Representatives, how should members vote? Do they have an ethical obligation to support the candidate who carried their state? Or the candidate who won the most votes nationally? Or perhaps the candidate of their party,

regardless of the will of the people? The 2000 presidential election would have been thrown into the House of Representatives had Florida's electors not been certified, thereby depriving both Vice President Gore and Governor Bush of an Electoral College majority. If the House had chosen the 43rd president, should such an outcome have been considered fair and legitimate?

5. Many of the elements of modern campaigns that are heavily criticized—negative personal attacks, overly long campaigns, the glamorization of celebrity candidates—were present in the elections of 1824 and 1828 as well. What does this reveal about the nature of political campaigns?

6. Undemocratic elements of our political system, from the Electoral College to the superdelegates used today in the Democratic party's nominating process to the unequal representation of the states in the United States Senate, endure. Why? What arguments can you make in favor of and against elements of our political system that grant more power to political elites and less to the people?

7. Are presidents, as Andrew Jackson claimed, truly more representative of the American public by virtue of their election by all the people than are members of Congress, who each only represent a narrow segment of the American people?

PART FOUR

JUDICIAL BRANCH

Search and Seizure and the Balancing of Rights—Mapp v. Ohio

PRISCILLA H. MACHADO ZOTTI

Courts cannot operate and justice cannot be rendered without evidence. Fundamental to due process is the principle that the evidence supporting the withdrawal of liberty be obtained and utilized lawfully. Therefore the very basis of a fully just legal system hinges upon the evidence it uses to make decisions. One important provision concerning evidence and the methods used to secure it is the Fourth Amendment. The application of search and seizure law in society provides a window into understanding rights and liberties enjoyed by all. Philosophically, the use of state power upon citizens, whether criminal or not, provides a yardstick by which freedom and liberty are measured. This case provides a perspective on rights and liberties useful in understanding the constitutional grants and limits of power typically presented in an introductory American politics course. It weaves together the story of Mapp v. Ohio *and its players, tracing the development of a legal remedy. From the underworld of gambling in Cleveland in the 1960s through the chambers of the Warren Court Justices, an obscure obscenity case becomes the vehicle for implementing the exclusionary rule.*

I KNEW THAT SOONER OR LATER I would receive a telephone call or email. I spoke with Mr. Carl Delau, or "Captain" as I fondly called him, every several months. We chatted and made small talk. He asked about my family. I inquired about his beloved dogs. But sooner or later we got around to reminiscing about *Mapp*. He would tell me a detail of the investigation, something he remembered. We discussed a point of law relating to search and seizure. For the police officer who was the lead on that Cleveland morning in 1957, *Mapp* had become a defining moment, at least in retrospect.

Cleveland 1957

Assigned to the powerful Bureau of Special Investigation, Sergeant Carl Delau was acquainted with Cleveland's vice activities. Horse racing and baseball belonged to the whites. Blacks controlled policy and gambling, although this was changing. Pornography was not a large problem, at least not yet. In May of 1957, Delau focused his attention on policy, or numbers wagering. The activities were located primarily in the 5th and 6th Districts of Cleveland and Delau was familiar with the principal players. Policy, or clearinghouse, was becoming big business in Cleveland. An illegal game of chance, policy appealed to those of all economic means. Even those with modest resources could regularly place a wager. They did so often. So much so that the Police Department of the City of Cleveland formed the Special Investigation Bureau headed by Lieutenant Martin Cooney. The Lieutenant was Sergeant Delau's direct superior. Cooney reported directly to the Chief of Police, Frank W. Story. Delau's chain of command indicated the importance the Cleveland Police Department placed on curtailing vice activities: Delau to Cooney to the Chief. The Chief of Police was determined to keep Cleveland from becoming a haven for criminals. He gave Cooney and his Special Investigations Bureau citywide jurisdiction.

About 3:00 a.m. on May 20, 1957, Sergeant Delau received a telephone call from a resident in the 4th District. He recognized the voice of twenty-five-year-old Donald King, a young but well-known clearinghouse operator who would later become nationally known as the boxing promoter with "that hair." King sounded desperate and bewildered. "Sergeant, they bombed my house."

"Donald, are you sure?" Delau asked King.

King replied, "I don't have a front porch. I can look out and it's gone. I don't have a front door."

Delau knew that King lived on East 151st Street, not far from the Mount Pleasant Police Station. "Did you call the police?"

"No," King said, "I called you first. You are the only one I can trust." He may have called Delau first but he had a suspicion who bombed his home. King placed a number of calls to others in clearinghouse and policy—others that he suspected were involved. He told them he was not scared and would talk to the police.

Within minutes Delau called in the report and was told to go to King's residence at 3713 E. 151st Street to investigate. There he found a clearly rattled Don King amidst the rubble that comprised the street-side portion of his home. By daybreak, fifteen officers were on site. King's residence, what was left of it, was a crime scene. What happened appeared to be a turf war for control of the policy business in Cleveland. Someone, using "muscle," was sending King a powerful message, likely another clearinghouse operator competing with King for business and power. Little did Carl Delau know, this was to begin the long chain of events that would forever change the way police conduct investigations in the United States.

The special unit that included Delau and his partner, Michael Haney, was established to combat the growing numbers games in Cleveland. The officers focused on two games of chance: clearinghouse or what was sometimes called numbers, and policy. Numbers and policy were played almost exclusively by blacks, primarily because the minimum bet could be as small as pennies and could be waged often, even daily. As Prohibition waned as a source of lucrative profit, whites turned their attention to gambling as a means of income. To do so meant driving blacks out of the business. The struggle for control took on interesting forms—raids, shootings, and bombings. (Roberts 56) Gambling was the leading "vice for profit" criminal business. The numbers were not trivial; the dollar amount, in the thousands per day. Both Delau and Haney became experts on these games of chance and each would often testify in court about how these forms of gambling were conducted. The special unit was successful in curtailing the rackets by keeping whites and the mafia from taking over an illegal activity dominated by blacks. Their job became twofold—keeping the peace between encroaching whites and black gamblers while snuffing out altogether games of chance.

There were very few operators who ran both clearinghouse and policy. The networks were too vast. There were six to eight clearinghouse operators and about eight to ten policy houses. For example, California Gold, Mound Bayou, T & O, S & G, Interstate all operated in Cleveland during the 1950s and early 60s. These games of chance were lucrative. One operator known to Haney and Delau cleared a profit of nearly $20,000 a day.[1]

At the epicenter of the Cleveland numbers and policy games was Alex Shondor Birns. Notorious in Cleveland for his use of "muscle" in the criminal community, Shondor Birns made a grand play to control policy. "Shin-do" as terrified blacks pronounced his name, was a white Jewish immigrant who was a legend in Cleveland for being tough, smart, and powerful. Birns, a dapper dresser often clutching an expensive cigar, looked like a gangster sent from central casting in Hollywood. It was hard to imagine Birns did anything else, with his wide lapels, expensive double-breasted pin-striped suits, and wide-brimmed fedoras. Birns looked like a gangster, not what you might picture as an executive of Cleveland's Union Supply and Towel Company, as he claimed.

Shon Birns played on the greed of competing racketeers by creating and organizing a system that allowed everyone to share in the profits. It also reduced the size of payoffs to winners by controlling the fluctuating odds. Numbers operators would often increase their odds in an attempt to lure business away from other operators. The result of such undercutting practices was often violence. Birns offered to "keep the peace" among the clearinghouses, control the odds, and cover any payoff that was too large for an operator to handle. This arrangement would curtail competition among clearinghouses and increase profits. Regulating the competition, providing insurance coverage for high payoffs, and control of the house odds came at a price. Birns would provide these "keeping the peace" services for 25% of the business. He was to be paid a weekly "fee" of two hundred dollars per operator per week. It seemed a small price to pay for some certainty within the gaming business.

One particular clearinghouse operator, Donald "The Kid" King had tired of the arrangement with Birns. In December 1956 he lowered his payment from the required two hundred dollars to one hundred dollars a week. By February of 1957 he had quit paying altogether. King felt that Birns did little for the money and that King could negotiate with the other clearinghouses himself. Birns services were no longer necessary

When Donald King lost his front porch early that May morning, he knew who likely would do such a thing. King immediately fingered Birns as the perpetrator. "Shondor was one of the five pistols who bombed me," King told the press.[2] King cooperated fully with the police, telling them that he was one of five clearinghouse operators who had paid Birns $200 a week. King had not paid Birns since early spring. He was out of the numbers business, he claimed. Donald King went on to name the four other numbers operators, Edward Keeling, Dan Boone, Buckeye Jackson, and Thomas Turk as possible suspects. He named Elijah Abercrombie as the person who collected the weekly money for Birns.[3] King told the police everything, not that they hadn't known about Birns and the others.

Less than three hours after the bombing, the police arrested Alex Shondor Birns at his Judson Avenue home. He told the police nothing more than his address, telephone number, and his place of employment, Union Towel and Supply Company on 34th Street. Birns, out of federal prison for only eight months, denied the charges saying, "I don't know these guys and I don't want to know them. They tell the police anything and the police believe them. I've got a job and a family."[4] Since Birns had returned to Cleveland, there had been two murders and seven bombings of policy figures (Roberts 87). Birns proclaimed his innocence, calling King a liar.

Carl Delau then arrested Keeling, Boone, Jackson, and Turk and took them to Central Station for questioning. The five were charged with blackmail on May 21, 1957, but the police had few leads other than their only cooperating source, Donald King. On May 25, 1957, the front page of the *Call and Post* blared the headline, "King Spills All to Cops: Blows Lid off Numbers 'Muscle.'"

Despite the overt threat, King did testify against Birns. Birns was brought to trial in October of 1957. Donald King, the star witness, spoke so quickly and in such animated form that the jury could hardly understand him. The press nicknamed Donald "The Kid" King, "The Talker," "The Mouth," "The Canary." On the witness stand, the defense attorney forced King to admit that he was a numbers operator as well as the owner of an illicit liquor store. King was the only witness, and not a particularly sympathetic one. The trial ended in a hung jury. The state decided to not retry Birns and the charges were eventually dropped. Later, it was revealed that Birns purchased the hanging vote of the jury for $8,000 dollars. To make matters even worse for King, the Internal Revenue Service promptly filed charges against King for nonpayment of taxes in regard to his gambling profits and placed a lien on his home. The house at East 151st Street was seized by the government as collateral for nonpayment (Evans). So Birns eluded any legal sanction while King, embarrassed, publically exposed, and now in legal trouble, faced jail time and financial woes for not paying Birns a mere two hundred dollars a week.

Numbers running was labor intensive. It required hiring people to make drop offs and pick ups, as well as book keepers, tabulators, look outs, collectors, and strongmen. The army of workers grew as clearinghouses became more and more profitable. Dollree Mapp worked occasionally for both Donald King and Shondor Birns, making drops, pickups, and sometimes keeping books. The police knew that she was involved in policy. When staking out known clearinghouses, they would regularly record license plates and later run them through the Department of Motor Vehicles's computer to obtain the names of the owners. Dollree Mapp's name had come up regularly. The police also knew her for her striking appearance. Dolly was a beautiful woman who Delau described as "foxy." She was tall, shapely, and dressed with flair, making her a standout in any crowd. Her appearance was striking. Even by today's standards, pictures of her show a beauty that is timeless. She was classically handsome and she knew it. Her looks took her a long way. Men, both white and black, found her attractive, and she took advantage of the opportunities these relationships provided her. She had some formal schooling, but her intellectual assets fell into the realm of street smarts rather than a bookish formal education. Her education had come from using her physical attributes and her quick wit to advance through those she knew. She was married once, to Jimmy Bivens, a professional boxer. She later became the girlfriend of Archie Moore, the famed heavy weight boxer who once fought Joe Louis. Dolly knew Shondor Birns well and years later referred to him with a softened voice as "Shon." Combining her physical beauty with her streetwise savvy, Dollree Mapp, while on the periphery, was a player in Cleveland's vice trade. For a black woman in the 1950s, she had made her mark. Carl Delau stated over thirty years later that she was one of the smartest women he had ever met.[5] He, on more than one occasion, called her brilliant.

Three days after the bombing of Donald King's home, Thursday May 23rd, Carl Delau and his partner, Michael Haney, were still searching for clues to link Shondor Birns to the crime. In the early afternoon, Officer Jackson of the Sixth District received an anonymous telephone call informing the sergeant on duty that one of the individuals the police suspected in the bombing, someone they wanted to question, was hiding out at 14705 Milverton Road.[6] The caller also informed Jackson that the police would find a large amount of policy paraphernalia hidden in the home (367 U.S. 643, 644). The information was passed along to Delau and Haney who were riding with Patrolman Michael Dever.

The address was familiar. The three officers left downtown Cleveland, taking Euclid Avenue near University Circle and Case Western Reserve University. Winding through Little Italy, at approximately 1:30 p.m., Delau, Haney, and Dever pulled their marked squad car in front of the home of Dollree Mapp. The car in the driveway was familiar too—it appeared to be that of Virgil Ogletree.[7] Ogletree had done time for numbers, extortion, policy, and clearinghouse. He was working with Keeling in numbers and had a reputation for conducting some of the more unsavory business of Shondor Birns. The officers did not believe that Ogletree bombed Don King's home but felt he could probably give them information which would assist them in finding out who did.

Delau and Haney parked and walked up the drive while Dever went to the front of the home. Delau rang the doorbell located near the side door nameplate "Mapp." Instead of coming to the door, the upper window near the driveway opened and Dollree Mapp coyly inquired what the officers wanted. Recounting this event in separate discussions over thirty years later, both Haney and Delau said, "I can remember her calling down from the window as if it were yesterday."[8]

Mapp continued to inquire, now more sarcastically, what Delau wanted in her home. Delau told her nothing concrete. After several more minutes of conversation she said, "I'll call my attorney and see if he thinks I should let you in." Mapp in fact did call the office of her lawyer, A.L. Kearns. Kearns was not available to speak to Mapp so Dolly was put through to one of his partners, Walter Green. Green was a relatively young lawyer whose specialty was not criminal matters and her request was not something with which he was readily familiar. "Do the police have a search warrant?" he asked. "I don't know. I didn't ask." she replied. "Well don't let them in unless they show you a search warrant, but if they do, you will have to admit them," counseled Green.

It turns out that Green's advice was not correct, at least not in the practice of American criminal law in 1957. While the constitutional principle of search warrant usage existed, the common practice under Ohio law was that search warrants were rarely used. Only when raids were planned well in advance were warrants considered. Most lawful searches occurred without search warrants. Green later recalled, "If I had known the way the law worked, I might have told her that she might as well open up the door" (Lieberman 283).

The Fourth Amendment to the United States Constitution reads: "The right of the people to be secure in their persons, houses, papers, and effects, against unreasonable searches and seizures, shall not be violated, and no Warrants shall issue, but upon probable cause, supported by Oath or affirmation, and particularly describing the place to be searched, and the persons or things to be seized." Despite the asserted need for a search warrant, the common practice in Cleveland and many other cities in the United States was to search without a warrant. If the police had enough clues and evidence to send them to a citizen's door, it was common to follow through on those leads. Delau and Haney had conducted hundreds of searches without warrants and their searches were routinely upheld in court as lawful.

The request by Delau and Haney to enter Dollree Mapp's home and search was not uncommon or extraordinary. It was not deemed outrageous or gross behavior. This was standard operating procedure for these two Cleveland cops. In fact, it was standard operating procedure for almost every local police officer in America. Nevertheless, when Dolly informed Delau and Haney that they would have to produce a warrant to enter her home, they set about the task of getting one. Warrants were not commonplace, but they were used. Carl Delau called Lieutenant Cooney and gave him the specifics. He told Cooney Mapp's home address and what they suspected to find inside, both in terms of the King bombing and clearinghouse materials. Cooney said he would take care of the warrant. Unbeknownst to Delau until much later, here was where the critical error was committed.

Lieutenant Cooney asked Lieutenant Tommy White to set about getting a warrant for Mapp's home. This entailed drawing up an affidavit which stated what evidence of criminal activity the police suspected would be found at the place or person to be searched. Warrants sometimes specified a person that the police suspected was at a specific locale. Other times an affidavit noted material evidence that the police wanted to obtain. The specific details would be laid out clearly in the affidavit. The affidavit was then presented to a judge. The judge, a neutral and impartial magistrate, would read the affidavit and determine if the police had probable cause, Probable cause, the legal threshold to support a search, requires an educated and reasonable ground that an allegation is well founded. If the standard is met, the judge then authorizes a search warrant to be issued, which is drawn up by a clerk, and given to the police. This procedure was not done regularly for many reasons. Occasionally a suspect was "tipped off" by someone that a warrant was being processed. The police would then show up to conduct a search only to find the criminals well prepared for their arrival, the element of surprise taken away. Some of the tip-offs were a result of corruption within city hall. Big city criminals were savvy and knew that clerks and administrative staffs had information vital to them. Salaries of police officers and other civic workers were low enough that bribes were tempting. What existed in Cleveland at the time was a culture of avoiding such steps, classifying them as an unfair advantage. Thus few in the police department knew how to obtain search warrants. When warrants were sought, Cooney typically asked Officer Ungarvy to obtain them. On this given day he was apparently unavailable and the job fell to Lieutenant White.

By about four o'clock in the afternoon, "Lt. White arrived on the scene with a search warrant."[9] Now there were at least seven police officers outside the Mapp house on Milverton Road. The officers on the scene proceeded accordingly. Again they sought admittance.

The fact that all parties had knowledge of a search warrant is uncontroverted. At the time the search was conducted, all the police officers involved believed that a search warrant had been obtained; Mapp's attorney, and initially, even Mapp herself: all believed that the police were operating with a search warrant. Ironically, no one thought to look to see if the piece of paper so commented on, so significant to future events and American constitutional law, was indeed a warrant to search 14705 Milverton Road, the home of Dollree Mapp. This act of omission is, without a doubt, significant. The very piece of paper at the heart of what would become *Dollree Mapp v. The State of Ohio* wasn't even scrutinized by any of the principal players. All took it for granted that the paper brought to the scene by Lieutenant White was an official search warrant to conduct a search of Dollree Mapp's home for a material witness in the King bombing and for potential possession of gambling paraphernalia. The trifold document remained folded, unopened, not read.

Dollree Mapp did not immediately answer the door, and the record reflects that at least one of the several doors to the house was forcibly opened. Carl Delau testified in court that "we did pry the screen door to gain entrance." Walter Green, Mapp's attorney, testified that a policeman "tried . . . to kick in the door" and then "broke the glass in the door and somebody reached in and opened the door and let them in." Mapp testified that "The back door was broken." According to Justice William O. Douglas's concurrence in the Supreme Court decision in 1961, "For the next two-and-a-half hours, the police laid siege to the house." It is interesting to note that the State's Motion to Dismiss before the high court states that "there was no evidence that any of the incriminating evidence was taken from the home of the Appellant by the use of any brutal or offensive physical force against the Appellant" (Motion to Suppress, State of Ohio, Supreme Court of Ohio).

At the time of their entry, Mapp was halfway down the stairs coming toward the front door. She demanded to see the search warrant, noting that the police had none on their earlier attempt at admittance. One of the officers, Lieutenant White, waived a piece of paper in Mapp's face, indicating that it was the search warrant which legalized their search. Mapp grabbed the paper and placed it down the front of her dress. The police then restrained her and recovered the so-called warrant. What is important to note is that *at the time* all believed the paper was indeed a search warrant. Only later was the existence of a warrant doubted. On May 23, 1957, everyone, including Dollree Mapp and Carl Delau, believed that a search warrant was the basis for the search of Mapp's home.

The police made a complete and thorough search of the four-room flat as well as the basement. In a trunk, materials deemed to be obscene were seized. This material was considered lewd and lascivious and when confronted, Mapp claimed she found the items while cleaning. She asserted that the material belonged to a former boarder, a Morris Jones. The obscene material included four pamphlets, several photographs, and a pencil doodle. In addition, Officer Haney found in her bedroom dresser "The Affairs of the Troubadour," "Little Darlings," "London Stage Affairs," and "Memories of a Hotel Man." Upon seizure of these items, Mapp replied, "Better not look at those; they might excite you" (Motion to Dismiss from State of Ohio). In a suitcase by the bed Officer Haney found a hand-drawn penciled picture (State's exhibits 5–9).

After the search and the seizure of the pornographic items, Mapp was arrested, taken to the police station, and jailed. Dolly Mapp would defend the possession of pornography by arguing it was not hers. She had rented out the spare room to a boarder (Jones) who was now residing in New York. Ohio law made this distinction moot. Mere possession of obscene material was punishable by seven years in prison. It did not matter that the possessor was not the owner, so Mapp's argument made little difference. Mapp was arrested and charged under Ohio Statue 2905.34 for possession of obscene material. "No person shall knowingly . . .

have in his possession or under his control an obscene, lewd, or lascivious book . . . print, or picture. . . . Whoever violates this section shall be fined not less than $200 not more than $2000 or imprisoned of less than one nor more than seven years, or both." Mapp was sentenced from one to seven years in the Ohio State Women's Reformatory and received bail for $2,500.00.

The Development of the Fourth Amendment

The Fourth Amendment, like so many other provisions of the Bill of Rights, was aimed at a specific, historical grievance. The events of the thirty years prior to the writing and passage of the Fourth Amendment are highly significant in elevating the principle of search and seizure to a constitutional right in American jurisprudence rather than continuing as merely legal principle. The use of the general warrant by the British antagonized the colonists and was central to the resulting urge and eventual break by the Colonies from the mother country. However, the law of search and seizure goes well beyond the few preceding decades of 1791.

Throughout the long history of search and seizure law, the dominant theme is that "a man's house is his castle" (Lasson 13). A right to be left alone in one's own home is universally recognized in the earliest of legal codes.[10] In ancient times, breaking into another's house at night could result in the death penalty (Davies 33). Roman law clearly delineated the privilege against search and seizure. Cicero said that one's home was a place of refuge sacred for all men despite the fact that searches at the time were very general and the authority to search was virtually unlimited. The searches, however, were broader than the seizures (Lasson 15). The origin of the famous maxim, "Every man's house is his castle," often credited to the English Lord Coke, is not an original English principle but one borrowed from the Romans. "*Nemo de domo sua extrahi debet*" (Lasson 15). Anglo-Saxon law reflects this Roman law influence.

Search and seizure law began to develop in England in the first half of the 14th century. It was dominated by disdain for the *general warrant*. These legal documents were issued by the ruling monarch and valid for the duration of his or her lifetime. It was not uncommon to arrest all suspected of having committed a certain type of crime and imprison them until further order by the King. The result of this general inquisition was a rather long imprisonment, two to three years not being out of the ordinary (Lasson 22). Objections to the Crown's methods of search and seizure were made particularly by printers, those accused of libel and sedition, and by merchants and others who were coerced by search and seizure to obey the tax laws.

Warrants were not specific; no person was necessarily specified, nor place. No oath was necessary to secure a warrant before a magistrate and no probable cause was required. The breadth of a search and the seizure which followed was determined by the holder of the warrant. In sum, the searching agent had free rein in carrying out his task.

General search warrants and writs of assistance were also used by the British against the colonists. The British regulated the importation of goods into the Colonies to raise money and to protect English industry. By 1761 the relationship between British customs houses and the colonists was tense, the custom officials using the writs of assistance and general warrants to search for smuggled goods.

In February 1761, all the writs of assistance expired due to the death of King George II. Sixty-three Boston merchants quickly petitioned the Courts of Massachusetts to address the validity of any new writs.[11] James Otis argued on behalf of the merchants, making an electrifying speech damning the use of general warrants (Taylor 36–7). John Adams, not yet a member of the bar and no more than 25 years of age, witnessed Otis's performance and marveled at his ideas. He recounted fifty-seven years later, "I do say in the most solemn manner, that Mr. Otis's oration against the Writs of Assistance once breathed into this nation the breath of Life.

Then and there was the first scene of opposition to the arbitrage claims of Great Britain. Then and there the child Independence was born. In 15 years, namely, in 1776, he grew to manhood, and declared himself free."[12]

In 1772, a group of Bostonians appointed a committee of twenty-one individuals to state "the Rights of the Colonists" (Lasson 72, n. 74). James Otis, in his last known public act, presented the report of the committee. One of the "Infringements and Violations of Rights" was the searching powers of custom officials (Lasson 72, 76–77).

The movement to codify the rights of individuals swiftly followed the Boston Committee. The colonists were intent on writing down in their early state documents their rights as they saw them being jeopardized by the British choke hold. At least seven states incorporated some personal freedoms and liberties into their constitutions.[13] The most notable of these for its similarity to the Fourth Amendment was the Virginia Bill of Rights written in 1776. Drafted by George Mason, who would later write portions of the Fourth Amendment, it was changed only slightly by James Madison (Lasson 79).

After the Virginia Bill of Rights was drafted, a search and seizure provision was written into virtually every state's declaration or bill of rights. Pennsylvania included in its Declaration of Rights the oath requirement to support the granting of a warrant (Poore 1542). Massachusetts' Declaration of Rights of 1780, Article 14, included the phrase "unreasonable searches and seizures."

When the First Congress met in June 1789 to write a Bill of Rights, the immediate evil addressed by the Fourth Amendment[14] was the general warrant. The original draft of the amendment, as penned by James Madison, contained only one clause, and it concerned the warrant. As it read, the intent of Madison's draft focused upon the warrant, not the search in and of itself. Madison and his committee colleagues saw the warrant as the *authority* for unreasonable searches and seizures (Taylor 41). Eliminating its flagrant use was the solution the drafters envisioned.

Madison's draft proposal was clear and straightforward. It recognized and constitutionalized an old common law tradition: namely, a right of the people to be secure against *unreasonable* search and seizure. It went on to provide that this right "shall not be violated" *by general warrants.* This was a direct response to the general warrants and writs of assistance crisis in colonial America.

> [O]ur constitutional fathers were not concerned about warrantless searches, but about overreaching warrants. . . . Far from looking at the warrant as a protection, they saw it as authority for unreasonable and oppressive searches, and sought to confine its issuance and execution in line with the stringent requirements applicable to common law warrants for stolen goods. The language of the early constitutions amply bears out these conclusions. . . . In all of them the warrant is treated as an enemy, not a friend (Taylor 41).[15]

The early case law of the Fourth Amendment focused on the reasonableness clause more so than the warrant clause. By 1914, the Supreme Court elected exclusion as the remedy for Fourth Amendment violations by federal searching agents. Why the Court selected exclusion as the favored remedy over others such as civil suit or the use of ombudsmen is unclear. In *Weeks v. United States* (1914) the Supreme Court ruled that the remedy for a Fourth Amendment violation by federal agents was exclusion. The *Weeks* ruling prohibited the admission into federal courts of any evidence illegally obtained. Some states adopted the new federal rule, or a limited version thereof; others utilized different remedies (Gangi 46–7). Police departments also made changes in their procedures for obtaining evidence.

Enthusiasm for the *Weeks* rule has had its limits. Counsel's efforts to get a *Weeks* exclusion in state cases were repudiated time after time, most vividly perhaps by the Roosevelt Court in *Wolf v. Colorado*, 338 U.S. 25 (1949). There the Justices were unanimous in holding that the security of one's privacy against arbitrary intrusion by the police—which is the core of the Fourth Amendment—is basic to a free society. It is therefore "implicit in the concept of ordered liberty" and as such enforceable against the States through the Due Process Clause [of the Fourteenth Amendment.] But, for the *Wolf* Court, *exclusion* of reliable, objective evidence was quite another matter. While the privacy right was deemed "basic to a free society," the *Weeks* remedy was not. The Court partitioned the right and remedy from one another, making one essential and the other not. This distinction, the majority found, not simply in its own value system, but in the practice of a great majority of the world's fifty eight English language jurisdictions.[16] Thus for the Roosevelt Court and most of the Anglo-American world—as seemingly for James Madison *et al.*—the proper remedy was to be found in the common law, supplemented by such legislation as the community might think appropriate.

In Cleveland, Dollree Mapp stood trial for violating the state's tough obscenity statute and was found guilty. She was sentenced to the Women's Reformatory in Cleveland. She remained free, out on bail, pending appeal. Delau and Haney continued to investigate policy and with the help of Donald King, would later charge Shondor Birns and his associates for the bombing. Cleveland was focused on the policy and gaming underworld. The trial of Birns and the star witness King were front page news. It appeared no one in Cleveland, except perhaps the local chapter of the American Civil Liberties Union, connected the legal developments of search and seizure law to the local events in Cleveland.

Walter L. Greene gave notice of appeal to the U.S. Supreme Court on June 15, 1960, three months after Mapp lost her appeal before the Supreme Court of Ohio. He raised six questions for review by the Supreme Court: The first two asked the court to decide if the Ohio obscenity statute was unconstitutional. This was A. L. Kearns's and Greene's original complaint before the Court of Common Pleas of Cuyahoga County. The third and fourth raised the questions of whether or not the sentence Mapp received was cruel and unusual. The last questions concerned the lack of review of the sentence by the court of appeals and state supreme court and the manner and content of charges made to the jury. The fifth question, whether it was placed in the list by order of importance or the order was more random, raised the legal problems resulting from the conduct of the police. "Did the conduct of the police in procuring the books, papers and pictures placed in evidence by the Prosecution violate Amendment IV, Amendment V, and Amendment XIV Section 1 of the United States Constitution; and Article I Section 1, and Article I Section 14 of the Ohio Constitution?"[17] A.L. Kearns and Walter Greene most likely wrote their appeal with the most egregious errors stated first and foremost. The Ohio Supreme Court's focus on the obscenity statute and the resulting split decision was, from their point of view, the best legal argument to set forth before the high court.

The Supreme Court Justices Hearing *Mapp*

Ascending as the Chief Justice of the highest court in the land on September 30, 1953, Earl Warren quickly found his voice among a court full of highly talented and vocal jurists. The Warren Court, as courts are often labeled by the moniker of their Chief, was a collection of some of the institution's most capable and strong-willed members. Yale Law Professor Fred Rodell labeled the Court "the most brilliant and able collection of Justices who ever graced the high bench together" (Rodell 284). Any law student or court watcher knows the names Frankfurter, Black, Brennan, Harlan. Even the lesser known members of Warren's court were strong, capable, and well accomplished.

The senior statesman of the Court was Hugo Lafayette Black. Born and raised in Alabama, Black was the first appointment to the Supreme Court by President Franklin Delano Roosevelt in 1937. Black's appointment to the high bench was briefly marred by his past. As a young man from 1923 to 1935, Black held membership in the Ku Klux Klan. The controversy stemmed more from the timing of the news of Black's association rather than the association itself. After his Senate confirmation, the national media reported Black's membership so widely that the newly appointed justice explained his membership and subsequent resignation of the Klan membership on national radio. Black's Senate years highlighted his allegiance to FDR. He spoke out and supported Roosevelt's New Deal programs and agreed with the famous court packing plan of 1936–1937. His overall record as a Senator prevailed and the controversy over his youthful association subsided.

Black's leadership on the court was not simply based on longevity. His southern drawl, droopy posture, and slight frame made it easy for others to underestimate him. Opponents, legal or otherwise, quickly found out this was a mistake. His intellectual tenacity spilled over to other facets of his life. Black was a competitive tennis player, whose devotion to the game was legendary. Even in retirement Black played several sets of tennis per day causing retired Justice Sherman Minton to say "The Chief calls me up once in a while and gives me a report on you and your tennis game. What a man! I can barely get around on crutches."[18]

Another Roosevelt appointee, who was different in almost every way possible from Hugo Black, was Felix Frankfurter. Born in Vienna, Austria, Frankfurter arrived in the United States with his parents in 1894, making his home in New York. His intellectual skills quickly took him to Harvard Law School where he excelled. He became a member of the Jewish elite of Boston involving himself in the Zionist movement. He regularly socialized and exchanged ideas with leading legal intellectuals such as Learned Hand, Benjamin Cardozo, Louis Brandeis, and Oliver Wendell Holmes, Jr. An original founder of the American Civil Liberties Union, Frankfurter was well known for his outspoken defense of Sacco and Vanzetti in the famous treason trial in 1921. Frankfurter met Franklin Roosevelt when the future president was Assistant Secretary of the Navy. In 1939, Roosevelt, after asking Frankfurter to serve as Solicitor General, a job he declined, asked him to be his third appointee to the high bench. Frankfurter remained an Associate Justice until August 28, 1962, just months after the *Mapp* decision was handed down and just prior to his eightieth birthday.

Of the nine, Frankfurter was the least capable of separating his professional position from personal opinion. His legal arguments, while sound, were in the end diminished by his lack of respect for those that disagreed with him. He cajoled and belittled the opinions of others who failed to adopt the logic that Frankfurter so eloquently set forth. Frankfurter's correspondence is full of criticism for his colleagues. The lines between legal reasoning in a professional setting and personal accord were often blurred. No doubt Felix Frankfurter was one of the greatest justices to ever serve on the Supreme Court, yet one wonders if he could have been even greater in impact if he had more tolerance for his colleagues and their differing points of view.

Another intellectual giant hearing the *Mapp* case was William O. Douglas. Douglas, a liberal who studied at Columbia Law School, was one of the original architects of the Securities and Exchange Commission, serving as Chairman in 1937. He was an early environmentalist, known for having helped saved the C. & O. Canal. His lifelong love of the outdoors stemmed from overcoming polio in his youth. He could be witty and acerbic all at the same time. He was persnickety. For example, he penned a memo to the chief that one of his secretaries is "slowly going blind because of poor lighting." He even advocated the creation of an escort service because a young female summer intern had to make her way alone when a guard refused to walk her to her car late one evening. Ever the supporter of the underdog,[19] Douglas, who began his lengthy court service in 1939, felt the need and duty to right a wrong, however small. For example, he wrote a terse letter to the Chief about his parking pass not being honored at National Airport once. After his health deteriorated as a result of a stroke, Douglas wrote a memo to the chief about the need for a whirlpool for his physical therapy. He insinuated that the Court should buy this for him so that he did not have to travel back and forth to Walter Reed Army Hospital and could therefore better serve the Court by receiving his treatment in house.[20] On court business Douglas made his decision with little concern of persuading or co-opting others. His sense was that the law was right and his job was to say so.

The last of the "*Mapp* court" to arrive in Washington prior to Warren was Tom Clark from Texas. Clark held to a philosophy of pragmatism and adherence to the rule of law. This pragmatism would prove crucial to the outcome of *Mapp v. Ohio*. Clark believed in obedience to the law and that cases should be only explicitly overruled, not overruled by implication. He believed it was within his right to dissent during the time in which the court had jurisdiction over a case, but once the case was decided, the decision should be supported until the time that a coalition was formulated large enough to overturn the outcome. This point of view was in play when *Mapp* came to the court since Clark had watched *Wolf* with dismay and only acted when he had a clear majority to change the law.

Several of the remaining justices who all arrived after Warren, while important to the dynamics of the court, were less important in the inner workings of *Mapp v. Ohio*. Charles Whittaker was nominated by Eisenhower to the high bench on March 2, 1957. He served on the court only five years. His beginning was humble, growing up in rural Kansas. Despite this, he rose to become a District Court judge and Eighth Circuit Court judge. Upon the advice of his doctor, Whittaker resigned due to physical exhaustion. He did not return to legal practice or public service. John Marshall Harlan, intellectual and cerebral, would be less important to the *Mapp* cases than in other areas of litigation. Harlan was Princeton educated, a Rhodes Scholar, and the grandson and namesake of Associate Justice John Marshall Harlan (1877–1911). Nominated by President Eisenhower to replace Justice Robert Jackson, Harlan was a solid force on the court who eschewed judicial activism and was less than enthusiastic of the Warren revolution. Lastly, Potter Stewart, Eisenhower's fifth and last Supreme Court appointment was likeable and a solid and able jurist. He, like his father, spent most of his adult life in public service in Cincinnati and in Washington.

To look retrospectively at the Supreme Court in the 1960–1961 term, is to see nothing startling. By the start of the new decade in 1960, Americans seemed hopeful of the things to come. The front page of the *Cleveland Plain Dealer* on January 1, 1960, discussed little that would concern the Court. On the heels of the decade of desegregation, the docket, while heavy, was the usual mix of cases. The number of docketed criminal cases was typical. The only unusual aspect of the Court's docket was its emphasis on communism. A rash of cases had made their way to the high bench concerning the liberties afforded those who disavowed democracy in favor of alternative forms of government. This issue consumed a good deal of the Court's docket as well as their intellectual energy. The precedential line of free speech cases, imprinted with the philosophical signature of Oliver Wendell Holmes, made headline news for the institution deciding such issues.

The *Mapp* case moved to the court with little fanfare. The briefs by all parties indicated the free speech debate over possessing obscene material was the only real issue. Ohio's strict statute attempted to set the legal bar high for possessing pornography. Merely possessing obscene material was a serious felony. This was no bombshell though. To the trained eye looking for landmark cases in the 1960 October Term, it was unlikely to focus on the case of *Dollree Mapp v. The State of Ohio*.

Mapp's dormancy on the Court's docket ended on October 24th. The Court noted probable jurisdiction with all of the Justices voting in the affirmative except for Felix Frankfurter. Frankfurter voted to dismiss the case outright.

The briefs in the case did little to crystallize the issue. Both Kearns and Mahon had focused on a variety of claims including the First Amendment, the Fourth Amendment, and Mapp's punishment. Concluded one of Warren's clerks, "The briefs of the parties in this case [*Mapp v. Ohio*] are among the worst I have seen all year. Happily, however, the amicus brief of the American Civil Liberties Union and Justice Taft's opinion in the court below tend to bring the major issues into focus."[21] Since the written word was not compelling, the oral presentations in *Mapp* would prove an important forum for the Justices to understand the case.

Oral Arguments

"Oyez, oyez, oyez, All persons having business before the Honorable, the Supreme Court of the United States are admonished to draw near and give their attention for the court is now sitting. God save the United States and God save this Honorable Court," so cried the Marshal on March 29th in the Court's beautiful marble courtroom. The confluence of events was about to be distilled into sixty minutes of legal argument. Dollree Mapp's claim was about to be heard in the highest court in the land on Second Street in Washington, D.C. "Case number 236 *Dollree Mapp versus the State of Ohio*," called the Chief Justice on March 29, 1961, at ten o'clock in the morning. Called to the podium first was A. L. Kearns, the lawyer that Dolly had tried to reach by telephone the day her house was searched, May 23, 1957.

Quickly and briefly, Kearns laid out the facts of the case. The issue concerning the search warrant was raised in moments. Kearns vindicated Delau by stating, "The evidence discloses that they were told that a search warrant had been procured."[22] Kearns calls the document a "supposed search warrant" and when pressed he says, "There was no search warrant, Your Honor. Now the evidence discloses that no search warrant existed, although they claimed there was a search warrant. There is absolutely no evidence of any magistrate that had been asked for a search warrant; there was no record of a search warrant. We asked during the trial of the case that the search warrant be produced and it was not. The fact of the matter is that our own supreme court found that it was very questionable as to whether there was a search warrant in this case."[23]

One of the Justices inquires, "What was the piece of paper? Did that get identified?"

Kearns: "We don't know what it was. She was not given an opportunity to read it."

Justice Frankfurter wanted even more specifics. "Are you asking us to overrule the *Wolf* case in this Court? I notice it isn't even cited in your brief. I just want to know what's before us, Mr. Kearns."[24] Kearns did not capitulate. Moving to safer ground, he explained in detail the Ohio statute and the consequences of the state Supreme Court ruling in terms of the First Amendment. This raised the issue of whether or not the statute was constitutional. Kearns interjected that also before the court was "the search and seizure proposition in this case." Asked Frankfurter again, "Well, that means you're asking us to overrule *Wolf against Colorado.*" Kearns' reply is significant for the later reach of the court. "No. I don't believe we are." Again, Kearns exchanged clarifying comments with the justices concerning what relief he was seeking from the court.

Court: Is the question that there was an unlawful search, is that in controversy in this case?

Kearns: No, it isn't.

The first sentence out of the mouth of Bernard Berkman seized the opportunity afforded Kearns. "I would like to say that the American Civil Liberties Union and its Ohio Affiliate, the Ohio Civil Liberties Union, is very clear, in response to the question which was directed to counsel for the appellant, that we are asking this Court to reconsider *Wolf versus Colorado* and to find that evidence which is unlawfully and illegally obtained should not be permitted into a state proceeding, and that its production is a violation of the Federal Constitution, the Fourth Amendment and the Fourteenth Amendment. We have no hesitancy about asking the Court to reconsider it because we think that it is a necessary part of due process."[25]

"Are you asking us to re-examine *Wolf,* or are you relying on *Rochin against California?*" asked the Court. Without hesitation Berkman replied, "We are asking the Court to re-examine *Wolf.* Our interest is not necessarily the same as that of the defendant who was convicted in this case, and our claim is more broad than that. . . ."[26]

The Chief Justice then called Gertrude Mahon to the podium. Arguing on behalf of the State of Ohio, Mahon gets off to a poor start. Justice William Brennan asked her if it is unlawful to possess obscene material, couldn't the clerk of the Court, the Court and even the prosecution be in violation of the Ohio statute? She replied no since the statute referred to unlawful possession such as possession with the intent to circulate. Brennan found her reasoning circular. "Your supreme court in this very case has construed this as meaning that if you have possession, naked possession, with knowledge that it's obscene, you're guilty of a crime under the statute."

Mahon: "That is right. But inherent in the element of possession is the opportunity for circulation, wouldn't you say, Mr. Justice Brennan?"

Brennan retorts: "It is not what I'm saying; it's what your supreme court is saying."[27]

Still unconvinced about what the statute meant by punishing for possession, Mahon is asked about book collectors. "On a bookshelf, merely as part of his library—he's a bibliophile and he collects first editions, not for the contents, but because it's a first edition. And any book on his shelves, on my shelves which I know to be obscene in content, but a matter of great indifference to me because I'm interested in the fact that it was published in 1527—that makes me a violator of the statute? Is that correct?"

Mrs. Mahon: "I would say so, Your Honor; any collector of obscenity would be . . ."

The courtroom broke out in laughter at the absurdity of her conclusion.

She finished her thought, ". . . would be violating this statute."

Frankfurter noted, "Well, Uncle Sam has one of the biggest collections [referring to the Library of Congress], and I can tell you now where it is, but it's outside of your jurisdiction."

The audience in the courtroom laughed again. The extremities of such a position weakened her core argument. She knew it, as did everyone else. If she stuck to her original argument of possession with regard to circulation, such rationale could hardly be applied to a book collector or a library's holdings.

The Court allowed her to ramble a bit, moving from the obscenity question and back again to the search and seizure question. It was clear she was not in control of the orals and was unsure of where a firmer position lay. For example, she flustered a bit with her position on the quality of the search and the exclusion of the evidence. "I have never been able to reconcile—that is, not reconcile; but it seems to me. . . ." Then she argued for maintaining the position the Court held in *Wolf v. Colorado*.

Just two days later, March 31st, the nine Justices met in their regular Friday conference to discuss the cases they had heard in oral arguments that week and to assign the writing of the majority opinions in each of them. When docket number 236 was presented, "The discussion continued to be devoted almost entirely to the constitutionality of the Ohio obscenity statute" (Schwartz 392). It was not difficult for the Brethren to come to an agreement on the state law. Justice Harlan's docket book reflects this consensus.[28] While there was widespread agreement on the state obscenity statute, there was considerable debate about the search and seizure question and the fate of *Wolf v. Colorado*.

Clark swiftly realized the opportunity *Mapp* provided. On the elevator after leaving the conference room, the Texan turned to Black and Brennan and asked, "Wouldn't this be a good case to apply the exclusionary rule and do what *Wolf* didn't do?" (Schwartz 393). The focus of Beckman's brief resonated. If indeed the search of Mapp's home was illegal, should the evidence be excluded? Was this the opportunity to change *Wolf*? Was this the case which would incorporate the remedy that corresponded with *Wolf*'s Fourth Amendment right? Clark was intrigued enough to consider the possibility. No doubt he found support in Brennan but the author of *Wolf*, Frankfurter, was horrified. On the question of search and seizure, Clark could rely on Warren, Brennan, and Douglas. He was one vote shy of a majority opinion which would adjudicate *Mapp* as a Fourth Amendment case. Still, the two-prong approach to Fourth Amendment violations could and would be revisited by the Court. Despite the lack of oral arguments on the matter, or briefs which fully explored the implications for the Fourth Amendment, *Mapp v. Ohio* was in the process of being transformed from a First Amendment obscenity case to a Fourth Amendment search and seizure case.

The core of Clark's opinion would not be altered much by his colleagues, but Clark was wise in attempting to build consensus for his draft. His request to Black was genuine. Indeed Clark's private papers reveal correspondence with Black and Douglas *even before* Clark released his first draft on April 28th. On April 25th Clark sent a note to Black, "Dear Hugo: I hope this is better. I have re-arranged and inserted new material. Thanks for the suggestions. TCC."[29] Clark's early drafts indicate substantial revisions and additions due to Black's input. A note of April 29, 1961: "Dear Tom: That is a mighty fine opinion you have written in No. 236-*Mapp v. Ohio*. Please join me in it. William O. Douglas."[30] Other justices too felt compelled to express their views. By early May, Clark had heard from Brennan saying that he would join. "May 1, 1961 RE: No. 236-*Mapp v. Ohio*, Dear Tom: Of course you know I think this is just magnificent and wonderful. I have not joined anything since I came with greater pleasure. Sincerely, Bill"[31] The Chief Justice joined as well. In a letter dated May 2nd the Chief writes simply, "Dear Tom: RE: NO. 236-*Mapp v. Ohio* I agree. E.W."[32]

However, both Potter Stewart and John Marshall Harlan indicated their reservations of Clark's early draft. Stewart responded on May 1st, "As I am sure you anticipated, your proposed opinion in this case came as quite a surprise." Stewart then laid out his concerns succinctly and forcefully. His writings indicate strong reservations. "In all honesty, I seriously question the wisdom of using this case as a vehicle to overrule an important doctrine so recently established and so consistently adhered to . . . I point out only that the idea of overruling *Wolf* was urged in the brief and oral arguments only by amicus curiae and was not even discussed at the Conference, where we all agreed, as I recollect it, that the judgment should be reversed on First Amendment grounds. If *Wolf* is to be reconsidered I myself would much prefer to do so only in a case that required it, and only after argument of the case by competent counsel and a full Conference discussion. Sincerely yours, P.S."[33]

On the eve of the historic decision being made public, it is interesting to note the path traveled by the *Mapp* case. Her trial and conviction, the appeals: all along the way she had lost. Each Court had found her violating the state obscenity statute. The only glimmer of hope lay in the interpretation that the state law making mere possession of obscene material a crime was over broad and vague. Mapp's best chance at winning appeared to be in declaring the Ohio statute unconstitutional due to its reach. Yet on June 15, 1961, Clark's opinion made little mention of the Ohio obscenity statute. He was prepared to hand down the most important search and seizure decision in United States history. Neither Dollree Mapp nor Carl Delau could have known that their encounter in 1957 would end up making headlines around the nation.

Aftermath

For Carl Delau, now a Sergeant on the Cleveland Police Force, June 19, 1961, was just like any other Monday. He paid little attention to the decisions of the high court and only discovered the ruling when he read it in the newspaper the following day.[34] The event was not a significant one, in the sense that he was not waiting anxiously to receive word from the high bench. He had paid no attention to the *Mapp* litigation. In his mind, the case was an obscenity question regarding the Ohio statute litigated in *Lindway*. *Lindway* focused on mere possession, which Mapp was certainly guilty of. His search of Mapp's home and the seizure of the evidence was not the central issue. For Delau, *Mapp v. Ohio* was an obscenity case, nothing more. He had not followed the case through the court system. When asked to recall any news coverage about the Ohio Supreme Court decision or the oral arguments before the Supreme Court of the United States, Officer Delau had none.[35] For him, the case held no real salience, although that was to change. If asked about the *Mapp* case before June 19th, Delau would have said something like the following: A known affiliate of local crime syndicates, Dollree Mapp was clearly guilty of possessing obscene material. Little mention had been made about the search and seizure of Mapp's home so Delau did not feel that his reputation was somehow being challenged. Only much later did the import of the decision come to bear.

Dollree Mapp, on the other hand, did watch the events in Washington with great interest. In an interview with the *Cleveland Call and Post*, she recounted her continual interest in the case. She and a girlfriend arrived by train in the nation's capital on a fall October day in 1960 to hear the oral arguments in her case. After finding a hotel that would accept blacks and taking in a few tourist attractions, she and her companion awoke the next day and went to the Supreme Court building. Dollree Mapp was in attendance for the oral arguments, seated in the public section of the courtroom, anonymous to the lawyers and justices. She told the *Call and Post* reporter that as she was leaving the courtroom at the conclusion of the oral argument, she met one of the doorkeepers and asked him when a decision was expected. He informed her that the Court often took months to decide cases. She then revealed to him that she was the litigant in the case just heard and that she was discouraged by the very long wait. She asked him if she could telephone him weekly to find out if there was a decision. He agreed. Each Monday she called. "Every Monday, I waited for the answer and they saved it until their very last session. I prayed for this! Then when it came, I fainted."[36]

The *Call and Post* article headlined her story with, "Must have Warrant Court Tells Police." Accompanying the article there on the front page was a photograph of Dollree Mapp, smiling, joyful, her face upturned and her hands clasped indicating her victory was sweet indeed. In her interview with the reporter, Bob Williams, Mapp sounded sophisticated and worldly, yet vulnerable. "I was in Kentucky on another case when my lawyers said they had a telephone call on the Supreme Court case. I had prayed for the answer that came, but when they told me the court had reversed my conviction, I just couldn't take it. The next thing I knew, they were reviving me. . . . It has been four years of torture and uncertainty. . . ."[37] The article was one of vindication for Mapp, always described as the "nationally known former wife of ex-boxer Jimmy Bivins and former girlfriend of Archie Moore, light heavyweight boxing champion."[38] Her future press clippings would not be so laudatory, but for now the limelight shone warmly on her. She was beautiful, a flashy dresser, and her dramatic interviewing flair made for good press. The court decision placed her center stage. Her name would become synonymous with other landmark court rulings such as *Miranda, Gideon,* and *Escobedo.* Any first-year law student knows of the plight of Ernesto Miranda, Clarence Earl Gideon, and Danny Escobedo. So, too, do they know the name Dollree Mapp. Dollree Mapp joined this group of infamous litigants, giving face to a landmark Supreme Court ruling that even in 2009 enjoys widespread notoriety. While her feeling of exhilaration dominated this particular Monday in June of 1961, she would later state that the decision and its accompanying fame created severe penalties for her.[39]

The opinion was reported in all the major newspapers around the country, usually on the front page. The *Cleveland Plain Dealer* led with the headline "Local Case Upsets Laws of Evidence." The *Plain Dealer* seemed more intrigued by the obscenity charge and the famous connections of Miss Mapp than the core ruling in the case. Calling her a "confidante of numbers racketeers, former wife of Jimmy Bivens, the boxer, and onetime friend of Archie Moore, the light heavy-weight boxing champion,"[40] the article went on to explain her conviction on the state obscenity charge. Indeed as the story continued on to the inside of the newspaper, the secondary heading read "Smut Ruling."[41] Mapp's attorney was quoted as claiming only partial victory, having hoped that the U.S. Supreme Court would overrule the *Lindway* decision and declare the Ohio obscenity statute unconstitutional.[42]

Effects on Case Law and Criminal Procedure

The *New York Times* gave the decision front page space on June 20, 1961, devoting much of the article to restating the major Fourth Amendment issues. "High Court Bars Evidence States Seize Illegally" was the headline. Little mention was made of the obscenity issue. The focus was overwhelmingly upon the *Wolf-Mapp* nexus and its impact on state criminal law. The case may be "the most significant limitation ever imposed on state criminal procedure by the Supreme Court in a single decision," argued the writer, Russell Baker[43]

The analysis followed the next day. The wonderful writer, Anthony Lewis, who would later pen the book entitled *Gideon's Trumpet,* about another famous criminal procedure case, *Gideon v. Wainwright,* wrote a detailed analysis of the *Mapp* decision. Having witnessed the oral arguments, Lewis focused on the broader issue of incorporation, applying portions of the Bill of Rights to the States. In this instance he was focused on the Fourth Amendment. In his article, "An Old Court Dispute," Lewis viewed the *Mapp* case through the lens of the chronic legal dispute of the piecemeal application of the Bill of Rights to state law. If this provision of the Bill of Rights was applied to the states, eliminating their choice of Fourth Amendment remedies (now it must be exclusion), what other portions of the Bill of Rights would be subject to the same application? Asked Lewis, "The question is what this (*Mapp v. Ohio*) signifies for issues aside from search and seizure."[44]

Lewis's eye was keen indeed, for the decade of the 1960s would see the Fifth Amendment self incrimination (*Malloy v. Hogan* 378 U.S. 1 (1964))[45] and double jeopardy clauses (*Benton v.*

Maryland 359 U.S. 784 (1969)); the Sixth Amendment right to counsel (*Gideon v. Wainwright* 372 U. S. 335 (1963)), confrontation of witnesses (*Pointer v. Texas* 380 U.S. 300 (1965)),[46] speedy trial (*Klopfer v. North Carolina* 386 U.S. 213 (1967)), and trial by jury (*Duncan v. Louisiana* 391 U.S. 145 (1968)) provisions; and the Eighth Amendment protection against cruel and unusual punishment (*Robinson v. California* 370 U. S. 660 (1962)) all applied to state criminal proceedings in identical fashion as in federal ones. *Mapp* was the inaugural of this criminal-procedure revolution. By the time Earl Warren left the high bench in 1969, little of the Bill of Rights criminal procedure provisions remained differentiated in state and federal courts.

The *Times* article surmised that "the search and seizure decision is expected to have sweeping effects on local law enforcement throughout the country."[47] Given the reaction of those in law enforcement around the nation, the media had keenly gauged their temperature. By July 2, 1961, the District Attorneys Association of the State of New York called on Governor Nelson Rockefeller to join them in seeking to overturn the decision in *Mapp v. Ohio.* One reason given was that the high court ruling would weaken the effectiveness of law enforcement to combat illegal narcotics trafficking.[48] In August 1961, the *New York Times* reported procedural changes in St. Louis due to lost arrests as a result of the *Mapp* decision.[49] The Court of Appeals in Albany, New York, attempted to establish a policy on the application of the *Mapp* decision on cases pending on the docket. The court, in adopting the policy, admitted "it would likely result in the reversal of many convictions in pending cases. . . ."[50] Across the country, judges and police chiefs tried to sort out what *Mapp* meant in terms of the legitimacy of current police practices. What kinds of changes were necessary and which would pass constitutional muster? Clearly guidance was needed, and shortly after *Mapp,* the Court would clarify the application of the exclusionary rule to a bevy of scenarios. The docket in 1962 and each year thereafter reflected this wave.

One hundred and seventy years after the adoption of the

Fourth Amendment, the Supreme Court of the United States via *Mapp v. Ohio* required exclusion in state cases. A high volume of litigation produced many similar exceptions to the requirement of a search warrant on the grounds that it was reasonable. The Justices allowed searches incident arrest, the most common of all, to be conducted without a search warrant because it was reasonable for the arresting officer to secure any evidence the suspect might have on their person and moreover, to ensure the safety of the police officer. Exceptions from the search warrant requirement were allowed for border searches, administrative searches, and logically, when the individual provided voluntary consent to be searched. The Justices wrestled with the particulars of automobile searches, allowing a generalized exception to the warrant requirement to stop an automobile but unsure about the status of the glove box, the trunk, and items inside the body of a vehicle. Did a search include the area surrounding an individual, that was "under their immediate control?" Could a police officer search without a warrant when in hot pursuit of an individual? The Justices took each of these questions, case by case, using what Justice Clark would term a "common sense" approach. The Court became a national review board, defining police procedure piecemeal. Those in charge of training and education in the nation's police academyies found themselves regularly digesting the latest search and seizure opinion from the high bench and trying to understand it in terms of its implications to the cop on the beat.

New York City Police Commissioner Michael Murphy stated that police departments had to "adopt new policies and new instructions. Retraining sessions had to be held from the very top administrators down to each of the thousands of foot patrolmen and detectives engaged in the daily enforcement function" (Murphy 941). By 1965, the Cleveland Police Academy reported the breakdown of class work and training for new recruits. Ten hours were spent on vice, policy, and gambling. Sixteen hours were spent on the rules of evidence (1965 Annual Report Cleveland Police Department).

Cleveland, Revisited

When spending time with Carl Delau, it is reasonable to believe that he was caught in a time warp. He searched Mapp like he did everyone else. He did not treat her differently. She was not singled out. What was different was the Court, the climate of change on the bench for the issue, and the opportunity to create the change. Delau operating under the status quo, his search of her in 1957 was like thousands of others. Based on the information Delau, Haney, and Dever had, they believed that Virgil Ogletree was in her home and he was somehow connected to the bombing of Donald King.

Of course our conversations always and eventually return to the search warrant itself. Why was White asked to get it? Why did Sergeant John Ungarvy, the police officer most familiar with search warrants not complete the task? He was in charge of getting warrants and typically did so for Cooney. When Delau called Cooney from the Mapp scene he told him he needed a warrant because Dolly demanded one. Cooney okayed the procurement of a warrant and, with Ungarvy not around, he gave it to Tommy White to do. White filled out the affidavit and took it to the judge, who signed it. However, White did not go back to the clerk's office with the documents. Herein lies the error. The typical procedure was that an affidavit was filled out and sworn to by the police. The judge would then decide if the warrant was supported with enough evidence, probable cause. If so, the warrant was granted by the judge and the officer then went to the clerk's office to get the actual warrant. Later, after the warrant was executed, the police returned it to the clerk's office who then filed it. This was typical procedure. White did all but go to the clerk, hence when he arrived at Milverton Road, he had with him only the affidavit. The crucial last step, converting the affidavit, signed by the judge and the police, into a viable warrant, had been overlooked.

When White brought the warrant out and handed it to Delau, Delau immediately went forward with a search and never ever looked at it. Back at the Central station, Delau opened up the paper to file it, seeing that it was an affidavit supporting a search warrant not the warrant itself. Delau did not panic. He thought perhaps Tommy White had left the warrant in the clerk's office. Delau and Haney went to Frank Hafee's office the next morning and with the help of the clerk looked everywhere, thinking that the warrant had indeed been procured but White had picked up the wrong piece of paper that he brought to Milverton Road. They checked in all the files and did not find it. When confronted, White said he was confused and eventually, sheepishly, apologized. Finally, it seemed that White never got the warrant. The clerk even offered to backdate a warrant for Delau and Haney: "I'll write it and back date it." "No thanks, wouldn't be right." Delau knew then that a search warrant had not been secured but it was too late. When the police told prosecutor John T. Corrigan, his reaction was to proceed as if they had it. Remember the warrant wasn't that important at this time; it was the pornography charges. So to Delau, Haney, Dever, White, and Corrigan, it was only a minor glitch because the focus was not on the search and seizure but on the felony charge of possession of pornography. According to Delau, Mapp never knew that at the time of the search, the paper he handed her authorizing their entrance was not a search warrant, but only an affidavit in support of one.

Dollree Mapp's possession problems no longer concerned obscene and lewd items but drugs. By 1968 she had moved from Cleveland to New York City. Located at 95th and Madison, Mapp operated a used furniture store in Harlem, Amsterdam Furniture. On November 2, 1970, Mapp was arrested in her St. Albans home in Queens County, Long Island. Police seized 50,000 envelopes of heroin and stolen property estimated at least $100,000. "The haul consisted of 10 television sets, 10 fur pieces, five electric typewriters, 11 portable radios, several sets of fine silverware, and an assortment of antiques, including clocks, vases, and candelabra."[51] The police also found a 3.5 kilo pure brick of heroin, scales for measuring, and quinine and lactose used in "cutting" heroin for street sale. Armed with a search warrant granted by Criminal Court Judge Daniel S. Weiss, the raid of Mapp's home was the result of an investigation by the narcotics unit. Mapp had been under suspicion for trafficking narcotics before. The November raid took place while she was out on bail awaiting trial for possession of almost a million dollars (street value) of heroin.[52] Arrested along with her was Alan Lyons, described by the police as her "youthful apartment-mate." Lyons, the manager of Mapp's furniture store, was considered to be the major player of the two and used the Amsterdam Furniture Store as a front for the drug operation.

On April 23, 1971, Dollree Mapp was convicted in New York State court and sentence to twenty years to life under a new and tougher sentencing statute enacted in 1969. She argued in court that the drugs, like the obscene material found on Milverton Road, were not hers. "It was a frame. I wouldn't be here if I wasn't black and I wasn't the Mapp in *Mapp v. Ohio*."[53] Her employee, Alan Lyons, was selling drugs unbeknownst to her. On May 26, 1971, she was sentenced to prison by Judge Paul Balsam and began serving her time at the Bedford Hills Correctional Institution for Women at Bedford Hills, New York. She later appealed her conviction on the grounds that the search and seizure of evidence from her home violated her Fourth Amendment rights. Her claim was denied.[54]

Epilogue

The telephone call I dreaded came in the form of an email in January, 2008. I received an email from Scott Brantley, a friend who is a retired Cleveland FBI agent who assisted me in my research. Carl Delau passed away at the age of 89 on January 12, 2008. He received full military honors including a riderless horse tribute and is buried in the Ohio Western Reserve National Cemetery.[55]

Notes

1. This entire section is the result of several interviews and correspondence with Officer Haney and Officer Delau. The interviews took place separately and it is amazing, despite the passage of time, the similarity of their statements.

2. *Cleveland Press*, Monday May 20, 1957, p. 1.

3. Cleveland Police Report filed by Sgt. Carl I. Delau, May 21, 1957.

4. *Cleveland Press*, May 20, 1957, p.1 "Birns is Jailed in Bombing Charge."

5. Interview with Carl I. Delau, Cleveland, Ohio, August 14, 1992.

6. Several sources mention that the anonymous call was from Dollree Mapp's boarder, Minerva Tate, who knew Officer Jackson. One police officer told the author that Don King was the source because he knew Dollree's tenant at the time, Morris Jones, and felt that he might possibly be involved in the bombing of King's home.

7. Virgil Ogletree's troubles did not end in 1957. He was arrested in 1992 on cocaine possession charges and sentenced to prison.

8. Interviews with Delau and Haney. Various dates in 1992, 1993.

9. This is the most critical divergence of facts. This statement is taken from the Motion to Dismiss from the brief of the State of Ohio in the Supreme Court of the U.S. The officers testified that Lt. White obtained a search warrant. According to Kearns, the officers on the scene were told that a search warrant had been obtained.

10. In addition, several passages in the Bible support the theme of the sanctity of one's home. See Joshua 7:10-26, Joshua 2:1-7, Genesis 19:4-11, Deuteronomy 24:10.

11. Only Massachusetts and New Hampshire passed laws allowing writs of assistance or general warrants to be issued. Other colonies struggled with the issue but, these were never culminated in law.

12. *Works of John Adams*, X, 247-248, in Lasson, p. 59.

13. Virginia, Pennsylvania, Maryland, North Carolina, Vermont, Massachusetts, and New Hampshire. The other six states either had no formal bill of rights or listed only a few. See Lasson, p. 82.

14. When drafted, the Fourth Amendment was the Sixth numerically in the list of twelve amendments presented to the states for ratification. Of the twelve, only the last ten passed, thus the Sixth numerically became the Fourth ratified. The Fourth Amendment as we know it was referred to as the Sixth Amendment in several early Supreme Court cases. See *Ex Parte Burford* 3 Cr. 448 2 L. Ed. 495 (1860) and *U. S. v. Bollman*, Fed. Cas. 14,6222 (1807).

15. Telford Taylor, *Two Studies in Constitutional Interpretation* (Columbus, Ohio: Ohio State University Press, 1969), p. 41. See, for example, the Virginia Bill of Rights of 1776, Clause 10, and the Massachusetts Declaration of Rights of 1780, Article 14. In Benjamin P. Poore, *Federal and State Constitutions* (Washington, 1877).

16. Frankfurter noted in his majority opinion in *Wolf* that only sixteen states had adopted the remedy of exclusion to address search and seizure violations, 338 U. S. 25 (1949); 75367 U.S. 643 (1961).

17. Notice of Appeal to the Supreme Court of the United States, *The State of Ohio v. Dollree Mapp*.

18. *Papers of Hugo Black*, Library of Congress, Letter September 11, 1964, from Sherman Minton to Hugo Black.

19. *Earl Warren papers*, Box 351, "Correspondence with WOD," Library of Congress Manuscript Room.

20. *Earl Warren papers*, Box 351, "Correspondence with WOD," Library of Congress Manuscript Room (memo dated in 1965).

21. *Bench Memorandum for Chief Justice Warren*, Box 210, Earl Warren Papers, Library of Congress Manuscript Room, Washington, D. C.

22. Transcripts of Oral Arguments, *Mapp v. Ohio*, page 1159.

23. Transcripts of Oral Arguments, *Mapp v. Ohio*, p. 1159–60.

24. Transcripts of Oral Arguments, *Mapp v. Ohio*, p. 1164.

25. Transcripts of Oral Argument, *Mapp v. Ohio*, p. 1170.

26. Transcripts of Oral Argument, *Mapp v. Ohio*, p. 1170.

27. Transcripts of Oral Argument, *Mapp v. Ohio*, p. 1178.

28. Found in the *Earl Warren Papers*, Box 356, Library of Congress Manuscript Room, Washington, D. C. In fact the docket books of each of the Justices reflects this similar understanding of the issues presented in the *Mapp* case.

29. *Tom Clark Papers*, Box A115, Folder 6, Tarleton Law Library, University of Texas at Austin.

30. Ibid.

31. Ibid.

32. *Earl Warren Papers*, Box 474, Library of Congress Manuscript Room, Washington, D. C.

33. *Tom Clark Papers*, Box A115, Folder 6, Tarleton Law Library, The University of Texas at Austin.

34. Interview with Carl I. Delau, various dates.

35. Ibid.

36. *Call and Post*, June 24, 1961, page 1.

37. *Call and Post*, June 24, 1961, page 2A.

38. *Call and Post*, June 24, 1961, page 1.

39. Interview with Dollree Mapp, March 15, 1993.

40. *Cleveland Plain Dealer*, June 20, 1961, page 1A.

41. *Cleveland Plain Dealer*, June 20, 1961, p. 5A.

42. *Cleveland Plain Dealer*, June 20, 1961, p. 5A.

43. "High Court Bars Evidence States Seized Illegally," *New York Times*, June 20, 1961, p. 1A.

44. Anthony Lewis, "An Old Court Dispute," *New York Times*, June 21, 1961, p 21A.

45. *Malloy v. Hogan*, 378 U.S. 1 (1964). Also clarifying state criminal procedure is *Murphy v. Waterfront Commission of New York Harbor*, 387 U.S. 52 (1964) and *Miranda v. Arizona* 384 U.S. 436 (1966).

46. *Pointer v. Texas*, 380 U.S. 300 (1965). See also *Washington v. Texas*, 388 U.S. 14 (1967) concerning the compulsory process to obtain witnesses.

47. "High Court Bars Evidence States Seized Illegally," *New York Times*, June 20, 1961, p. 1A.

48. *New York Times*, July 2, 1961, p. 24A.

49. *New York Times*, August 6, 1961, p. 30A.

50. *New York Times*, December 1, 1961, p. 21A.

51. *Call and Post*, Saturday, November 7, 1970, p. 1A.

52. Ibid.

54. *Dollree Mapp and Alan Lyons v. Warden, New York State Correctional Institution for*

Women Bedford Hills, New York and Warden, Great Meadow Correctional Facility, Comstock, New York, 531 F.2d 1167, United States Court of Appeals for the Second Circuit, (March 16, 1976).

55. Much of this essay is excerpted from the book by the author, *Injustice for All: Mapp vs. Ohio and the Fourth Amendment*, New York: Peter Lang Publishing, 2005.

References

Annual Report of the Cleveland Police Department, 1965.

"Birns is Jailed in Bombing Charge." *The Cleveland Press.* 20 May 20, 1957: 1.

Cleveland Call and Post, various dates.

Cleveland Plain Dealer, various dates.

Cleveland Press Newspaper, various dates.

Davies, W. W. *Code of Hammurabi and Moses.* Cincinnati, Kessinger Publishing, 1915.

Delau, Carl. Personal Interview, Various Dates, 2000–2008.

Earl Warren Papers, Library of Congress Manuscript Room, Washington, D.C.

Evans, Christopher. "The Man Who Would be King," *Cleveland Plain Dealer Magazine,* October 23, 1988.

Felix Frankfurter Papers, Harvard Law School, Manuscript Collection, Boston, Massachusetts.

Gangi, E. "The Exclusionary Rule: A Case Study in Judicial Usurpation," *Drake Law Review* 34.33: 46–47 (1984).

Haney, Michael. Personal Interview, Various Dates 1992–1993.

Lasson, Nelson B. *The History and Development of the Fourth Amendment to the United States Constitution.* Baltimore: Johns Hopkins University Press, 1937.

Lieberman, Jethro K. *Milestones: 200 Year of American Law.* New York: Oxford University Press, 1976.

Mapp, Dollree. Personal Interview, Various Dates 1992–1998.

Mapp v. Ohio, 367 U. S. 643 (1961).

Murphy, Michael. "Judicial Review of Police Methods in Law Enforcement: The Problem of Compliance by Police Departments," *Texas Law Review.* 44, 941 (1966).

Papers of Hugo Black, Library of Congress Manuscript Room, Washington, D.C.

Roberts, Michael. "Why They Blew Shondor Birns Away," *Cleveland Magazine.* July/December, 1975.

Rodell, Fred. *Nine Men: A Political History of the Supreme Court from 1790 to 1955.* New York: William S. Hein and Co., 1988.

"Six Defendants Whose Cases Changed American Law," *People Weekly,* 5 May 1975.

Taylor, Telford. *Two Studies in Constitutional Interpretation.* Columbus, Ohio: Ohio State University Press, 1969.

Tom Clark Papers, Tarleton Law Library, The University of Texas at Austin.

Zotti, Priscilla H. M. *Injustice for All: Mapp vs. Ohio and the Fourth Amendment.* New York: Peter Lang Publishing, 2005.

Questions

1. Was it appropriate for the Supreme Court of the United States to use a pornography case as a vehicle for the Fourth Amendment change? Should they have waited for a search and seizure case? Should they have only ruled on the Ohio obscenity statute or is it in their purview to broaden the scope of a legal question?

2. Did the right to be protected against unreasonable searches and seizures emerge by actions of the Justices of the Supreme Court or did the right exist through the history and development of the Fourth Amendment? How important is the intent of the framers when considering the rights contained in the Constitution?

3. Exclusion is a bright line rule, meaning that the rule is very clear: illegality on the part of the police always triggers exclusion. There is no other option. Illegally obtained evidence is excluded from use by criminal courts. Does such a windfall to those who are accused tip the balance between liberty and authority unjustly? What is the proper balance?

4. What is appropriate for courts to do? Should they only react to what the legislature does by way of a statute or can they reach out, such as they did in *Mapp*, and go beyond the statute in question?

5. Fundamental to the Fourth Amendment is the nexus between rights and remedies. Since the Amendment specifies a right without specifying a remedy, is it appropriate for courts to determine that remedy or should state legislatures do this?

6. Our Constitution protects the rights of those accused of crimes through the Fourth, Fifth, Sixth, and Eighth Amendments with little or no mention of the rights of victims. Should we as a society be so concerned about the rights of those accused of being lawbreakers?

7. Evidence is crucial for the state to convict those accused of crimes. However, the exclusionary rule eliminates probative information because of a procedural error by the police. How important is procedural integrity versus result?

8. Ultimately *Mapp v. Ohio* is about the balance between liberty and authority. How best should we achieve this balance in the face of rising crime and terrorism? Consider, for example, the Patriot Act and its content.

9. Dollree Mapp benefitted by a change in constitutional interpretation

that took place in 1961. How much of a role did timing of court personnel and agenda play in her victory? What does that say about constitutional interpretation?

10. Who is the victim in *Mapp v. Ohio*, Dollree Mapp or Carl Delau? Explain.

11. How best can we balance the rights of the accused with the rights of the state to investigate, gather evidence, and seek convictions? Does the exclusionary rule achieve this balance?